FLORIDA HOSPITAL *Healthcare & Leadership* MONOGRAPH SERIES

MONOGRAPH VOLUME III

Music, Medicine & Miracles

HOW TO PROVIDE MEDICAL MUSIC THERAPY FOR PEDIATRIC PATIENTS AND GET PAID FOR IT

AMY ROBERTSON, MM, MT-BC, NICU MT

Florida Hospital
for Children

FLORIDA HOSPITAL
HEALTHCARE
&LEADERSHIP
MONOGRAPH SERIES

MUSIC, MEDICINE & MIRACLES
Copyright © 2009 Amy Robertson
Monograph Volume 3
Published by Florida Hospital
683 Winyah Drive, Orlando, Florida 32803

TO EXTEND *the* HEALTH *and* HEALING MINISTRY *of* CHRIST

GENERAL EDITOR	Todd Chobotar
PRODUCTION EDITOR	Sarah Hayhoe
COPY EDITOR	Debbie Upp
EXTERNAL PEER REVIEW	Jayne Standley, PhD, MT-BC, NICU-MT
	Darcy Walworth, PhD, MT-BC, NICU-MT
INTERNAL PEER REVIEW	John Edwards, MD
	Jennifer Beckner, RN
PROMOTION	Stephanie Rick
PROJECT COORDINATION	Lillian Boyd
PHOTOGRAPHY	Spencer Freeman
PRODUCTION	Carter Design, Inc.

PUBLISHERS NOTE: This monograph is not intended to replace a one-on-one relationship with a qualified health care professional, but as a sharing of knowledge and information from the research and experience of the author. You are advised and encouraged to consult with your health care professional in all matters relating to your health and the health of your family. The publisher and author disclaim any liability arising directly or indirectly from the use of this monograph.

AUTHOR'S NOTE: This monograph contains many case histories and patient stories. In order to preserve the privacy of the people involved, I have disguised their names, appearances, and aspects of their personal stories so that they are not identifiable. Patient stories may also include composite characters.

Library of Congress Cataloging-in-Publication Data
Robertson, Amy
Music, Medicine & Miracles / by Amy Robertson
p. cm.
1. Music – Medical aspects. 2. Music Therapy – Physiological aspects
3. Health – physical, emotional, spiritual. I. Title
ISBN-13: 978-0-9820409-2-8
ISBN-10: 0-9820409-2-x

Printed in the United States of America
FP 10 9 8 7 6 5 4 3 2 1

For volume discounts please contact special sales at:
HealthProducts@FLHosp.org | 407-303-1929

For more resources on Whole Person Health please visit:
FloridaHospitalPublishing.com

CONTENTS

EDITOR'S INTRODUCTION

SPEAKING OF HIS PROFESSION, ELVIS PRESLEY once remarked, "I don't know anything about music. In my line you don't have to." A funny statement coming from one of the best-selling musicians in history? Definitely. Then again, how much do any of us really know about music? Yes, we may have favorite songs, styles, and artists, but does that mean we really know music? Some of us can read or write music, play an instrument, or sing a melody. But does that mean we understand it?

In truth, music defies easy definition. It is both obvious and a mystery. A universal language and a highly personal experience. Music affects us in ways difficult to describe and even harder to quantify. Yet it has power. Power to move us, motivate us, console us, humble us, inspire us, and perhaps even heal us.

Over the last half century a growing body of research points to the medicinal effects of music on the human body. Effects practiced and fine-tuned by the growing field of music therapy. In these pages, Amy Robertson takes us on a journey into the world of pediatric music therapy. With an outstanding mixture of clinical vignettes, scientific information, and practical administrative experiences, she presents a compelling case for creating music therapy programs for infants and children across the country. I believe any hospital – especially any children's hospital – can benefit from using this monograph to enhance its services.

Ms. Robertson has written a hands-on, experience-based guide for incorporating music therapy into the current cost-conscious hospital environment. The thoroughness with which the subject is addressed is a real strength. Her success in building the program at Florida Hospital for Children and her journey through the maze of medical coding, billing, and reimbursement will prove invaluable to music therapists, hospital administrators, physician leaders, and clinical staff at any healthcare facility.

Perhaps Elvis, you, and I don't know much about music. But we can learn. We can learn to harness its power so that some day music, medicine, and miracles can help bring health and healing to us all.

Todd Chobotar, General Editor

FOREWORD

MUSIC HAS A PROFOUND EFFECT ON OUR EMOTIONS and psyche. This is not really news. Music makers and music lovers have known it for millennia. What is news is that in the last 50 years modern medicine has discovered many of the beneficial effects of music on the physical body. With this discovery, the discipline of medical music therapy arose to employ music as an instrument of healing. Today music therapy is an evidence-based healthcare profession that research has shown effective with a wide range of populations in the hospital setting.

Using various music interventions, music therapists can decrease anxiety and depression, increase coping skills and even stabilize blood pressure and respiration rates.

Even though music therapy can be effective from first cry to last breath, it has a profound effect on hospitalized children. In the last ten years, research has shown that premature infants are able to leave the hospital significantly sooner with music therapy. In some cases, children undergoing procedures like echocardiograms and CT scans are using music therapy instead of sedation. But despite these desirable applications and outcomes music therapy is not as widely accepted and used as it could be.

In a world where healthcare costs continue rising and budgets continue falling, it is becoming harder to implement programs that focus on holistic approaches to healing such as music therapy. Currently, many of these programs are supported by grants and endowments. If these resources aren't available, many healthcare institutions are not able to implement these life-changing professional services.

Perhaps that's the reason I'm so excited about this monograph from Amy Robertson. Ms. Robertson has taken her experience of starting a music therapy program from scratch at the largest admitting hospital in America and provided step-by-step instructions on how others can do the same. Her insights on implementing a cost-effective music therapy program are invaluable. Further, she demonstrates that in addition to the health and healing benefits music therapy provides it can also bring cost-savings and reimbursement to hospitals.

Ms. Robertson became the first in the country to successfully receive reimbursement for inpatient services in the NICU. In this monograph she not only explains how she accomplished this, but how others can as well. Her contributions have broken some boundaries for music therapy and created new opportunities for therapists to continue healing the mind, body, and spirit with music.

I am encouraged by *Music, Medicine & Miracles*. Ms. Robertson is both clinically sensitive and administratively astute. Her work is skillful, practical and long overdue. I believe that it will open wide the doors of acceptance for the treasure we bring as music therapists. I applaud her exceptional efforts on a much needed monograph and hope the insights presented here will persuade everyone from doctors, nurses, hospital administrators, students, patients and their families to take a closer look at the remarkable benefits of music therapy.

Ms. Robertson's enthusiasm to integrate music therapy into the care of every pediatric patient in need is a passion we can all share. Please add my name proudly to the supporters of Ms. Robertson's work – and hurry – the public awaits!

Deforia Lane, Ph.D., MT-BC

Director of Music Therapy

Associate Director Ireland Cancer Center

University Hospitals Health System

Author of *Music As Medicine*

MUSIC, MEDICINE & MIRACLES

I COULD TELL BY THE LOOK on the nurse's face she was flustered. She'd spent most of the day trying to calm down Baby Mason. He cried constantly and didn't like to be held or taken out of his crib. He was admitted to the Florida Children's Hospital Neonatal Intensive Care Unit (NICU) not only for being premature, but for exposure to addictive drugs in utero. His neonatal physician ordered music therapy to attempt to increase Mason's tolerance of the hospital environment by using multimodal stimulation.

When I received the Music Therapy (MT) order, my colleague and I met with his nurse who told us we shouldn't hold him and it would probably be best to provide the multimodal stimulation while he was in the crib. Normally, most people are hesitant to stimulate this type of infant, but I knew a simple lullaby might just do the trick. Mason was a little fussy when we walked into the NICU. My colleague prepared her guitar and I asked her to begin playing.

> As the first lullaby began, Mason stopped squirming and looked in the direction of the guitar. I started to sing a soft lullaby and he looked at me expressing a small smile. So far so good, I thought. Even after a few minutes, he remained still continuing to look all over as we kept softly singing. At this point, I wanted to try providing the multimodal stimulation treatment because I knew it would help increase his tolerance to the world around him.

Turning to the nurse, I asked if I could try holding him. She saw he was calm, and hesitantly said, "You can try, but if he starts crying you're going to need to put him back in the crib and stop for the day." I sat down in the chair next to his crib. As the nurse picked him up, he began to protest. When she put him in my arms, I leaned my head down, made eye contact with him and continued to sing the lullabies. He stopped fussing and became comfortable again.

After a few more minutes, I started to provide the massages that are a part of the multimodal stimulation treatment. I began on the top of his head slow and purposefully making my way through the progression. Mason's eyelids grew heavy; he started to close them. During the treatment, he startled a few times, but for the most part remained calm and comfortable. The nurse kept returning every few minutes to make sure he was ok and said, "Wow, I think he likes the music." When we finished, she came back in and said, "I think the music really worked. He usually never lets anyone hold him."

As we continued to see Mason, he progressed through the treatment and eventually was able to tolerate auditory (sound), tactile (touch) and vestibular (movement) stimulation all at once. The nurses commented at how well he did during music and how he was a happier baby.

While some premature infants are able to develop with little or no difficulty, many experience problems that will last throughout their stay in the NICU and even the rest of their lives. Premature infants frequently experience a wide variety of medical problems such as underdeveloped organs, visual and digestive problems, and bleeding of immature brain tissue. They can also experience servomotor conditions like cerebral palsy along with behavioral problems and learning disabilities. These challenges can create overwhelming and difficult circumstances for the infants and parents. These infants are also easily over-stimulated by the sights and sounds of the NICU environment. At a time when they are supposed to be in the quiet, safe environment of the mother's womb, they are being picked up, cuddled, changed and talked to by their parents and clinical staff, overloading their neurological system, resulting in stress behaviors such as crying.

When premature infants are exposed to drugs while in the mother's womb, they not only have to deal with the common medical problems from being premature, but they often have to endure withdrawal. Premature infants who are suffering from withdrawal are sometimes agitated and easily become over-stimulated. Parents of these infants face the challenge of trying to stop drug use, which takes time away from the infant and provides for limited bonding time.

DEFINING MUSIC THERAPY

MEDICAL MUSIC THERAPY MUST BE well defined to truly understand, not only what it is, but what it is not. Music therapy is the prescribed use of music by a qualified person to effect positive changes in the psychological, physical, cognitive, or social functioning of individuals with health or educational problems.

Music therapy is an evidence-based practice using music and music techniques to achieve non-musical goals. It can enhance well-being and increase quality of life for those who are well and meet the needs of those with illnesses or disabilities. Every technique used by music therapists has been proven effective first through research. From premature infants to older adults, studies have shown that music therapy interventions have been significantly beneficial to people of all ages and diagnosis.

Since ancient times, music has been used to treat diseases and cure physiological and psychological illnesses. Reports from the late 1800's found that music was being used to treat physiological processes such as blood pressure, heart rate, cardiac output, and respiratory rate. The current discipline began after World War I and World War II, when amateur and professional musicians were found in VA hospitals around the country attending to wounded soldiers who were suffering from physical and emotional trauma. The noticeable effect that the music had on the veterans led to nurses and doctors requesting that the hospitals hire musicians. As demand grew, it became evident the musicians needed training prior to entering the hospital environment and a college curriculum needed to be created. The first university program for a music therapy degree was established in 1944 at Michigan State University. Today more than seventy-five degree programs exist in the United States alone. In 1998, the *National Association for Music Therapy and the American Association for Music Therapy* joined and established the *American Music Therapy Association*, the current governing body for music therapists practicing in the United States.

Medical Music Therapy differs from other stimuli-related styles including harp therapy, music thanatology, Artist-in-Residence and Arts-in-Medicine programs, though each has been confused with music therapy in the past. Medical Music Therapists obtain a four-year degree from an accredited university. Required coursework for music therapists includes music performance and theory, psychology, science, anatomy and physiology, history, statistics and research – a curriculum that closely resembles degrees in psychology. Master's and doctoral level programs are also available in music therapy. Once music therapy students have completed coursework for their bachelor's degree, they must complete a 1000-hour internship before they are eligible to sit for the national examination offered by the Certification Board for Music Therapists. Music therapists who successfully pass the independently administered examination hold the credential of Music Therapist Board-Certified (MT-BC).

Music therapists are uniquely trained and qualified in using music to practice evidence-based therapy and research with all patient and client populations. While music therapy in no way negates the value of complementary programs, it is important not to confuse those programs with music therapy since the training, treatment goals, research and results are quite different. Given their training and credentialing, music therapists are rightly held to a higher standard of measurable medical results.

A music therapist is not merely a musician, but rather a clinician trained to achieve medical objectives through the expert use of music. This differentiation is crucial to understanding the value of music therapy in practice, especially when working with fragile populations such as premature infants. Figure 1 describes the common complimentary programs that are often confused with music therapy and the training needed for each.

MUSIC PROGRAMS SOMETIMES CONFUSED WITH MEDICAL MUSIC THERAPY		
PROGRAM	SERVICES	EDUCATION
Harp Therapy	Harp therapy is a non-research based practice in which the therapists play the harp at bedside to offer the recipient comfort, release of emotions and relaxation. Usually harp therapists play at hospice facilities or any place that deals with end-of-life care.	For a person to become a harp therapist, they must be certified. This includes classroom hours, a practicum project, readings, writings and a 100-hour closely supervised internship. Qualifications for Certified Master of Harp Therapy include all of the same requirements, as well as an additional 100-hour internship. Over 50% of the classroom studies required for the certification consists of musical and repertory development.
Music Thanatology	Music Thanatology is a field in which the practitioners provide comfort through the harp and voice at the bedside for patients near the end of life.	The music thanatology training program is a non-degree program that consists of 2 years of training and 300 hours of patient contact time.
Arts-In-Medicine Affiliated	Arts-in-Medicine is a partnership between a local university and a hospital in which volunteers provide services to enhance the aesthetic environment of the hospital. Students are able to interact with patients at bedside through a variety of activities including, but not limited to: playing cards, coloring (pediatric patients), reading books, playing games, doing arts and crafts, or simply making conversation.	Students of any degree program can enroll for the course and depending on how many hours the students sign up for dictates the number of volunteer hours at the hospital.
Artist / Musician-In-Residence	An Artist/Musician–in–Residence program consists of trained artists and volunteers that bring art to the bedside to provide a positive diversion for hospital patients. This type of service helps patients express themselves through art and other modalities such as music, poetry and storytelling.	This type of program usually consists of artists who are paid by the hospital to provide services to patients or an artist-in-residence coordinator who provides education and training for volunteers. The Artist/Musician–in–Residence has knowledge and/or an educational background in art or art therapy.

Figure 1

POPULATIONS WHO BENEFIT FROM MUSIC THERAPY

E VEN AFTER YEARS OF FULL-TIME PRACTICE, my title of Board Certified Music Therapist still elicits demeaning – though well-intentioned – comments such as, "Oh, that's nice. How often do you volunteer at the hospital?"

The truth is our team of therapists is responsible for a wide variety of clinically important outcomes including the reduction of pain, anxiety, and depression for most patient populations in the hospital. Music therapy interventions achieve many desirable outcomes from managing pain to stimulating sensory and mental cognition. Through the use of prescribed music, Board-Certified Music Therapists strive to effect positive changes in the physical, psychological, cognitive, or social functioning of patients with health or educational problems.

With a legacy of over 50 years, the practice of music therapy has contributed to successful healthcare in a way that is attracting increased notice and respect within the medical community.

Music therapy has been proven, in many patient populations, to stabilize heart rate,[1] respiration rate,[2] and blood pressure,[3] increase oxygen saturation levels,[4] and decrease cortisol levels[5] and the need for medication.[6] It has been shown to increase the coping skills and quality of life for cancer patients.[7] For patients in the Intensive Care Unit (ICU), music therapy can increase relaxation and help stabilize vital signs such as respiration rates.[8] It helps normalize the hospital environment for children[9] and can decrease or eliminate the need for sedation for certain pediatric procedures.[10] It can also increase the tolerance of premature infants to the NICU environment, sending them home

USES AND GOALS OF MEDICAL MUSIC THERAPY

+ Promote movement for physical rehabilitation
+ Increase receptive and expressive speech due to neurological disorders
+ Increase sensory stimulation, usually in patients that have had a stroke or have been in a coma
+ Pain management
+ Decrease anxiety
+ Counteract depression
+ Increase quality of life
+ Elevate mood
+ Increase relaxation
+ Counteract negative thoughts or fears
+ Improve reality orientation
+ Increase coping skills for illness
+ Stress management
+ Cognitive stimulation
+ Eliminate need for sedation
+ Socialization
+ Increase motivation
+ Increase communication
+ Normalize environment

Figure 2

an average of 12 days sooner;[11] earning many hospitals (including Florida Hospital for Children) thousands of dollars a year and saving at least $250,000 annually due to NICU MT services alone. (See figure 2 for a list of music therapy uses and goals.)

Music therapists can achieve these outcomes in multiple settings including schools, mental health centers, rehabilitation clinics, nursing homes, correctional facilities, and hospitals.

Music therapy has met particular success with premature infants in Neonatal Intensive Care Units (NICU) and has had profound effects in working with children undergoing stressful procedures. The scope of this monograph encompasses the research, effects, and success of music therapy with premature infants and music therapy assisted pediatric procedures. It will also cover recent insurance reimbursement received through the NICU music therapy program with details about how to start and fund such a program at any healthcare facility working with premature infants and young children.

The aim of this monograph is also to empower healthcare administrators and clinical staff to collaborate with music therapists to achieve the benefits of a pediatric and NICU music therapy program, while providing music therapists a guide for program development and implementation. Research in the NICU area has shown music therapy to be a safe, non-invasive treatment for premature infants resulting in shorter length of stay, quicker weight gain, and overall better tolerance to the NICU environment. During the last decade, music therapists have been implementing specialized techniques to assist with pediatric procedures to increase distraction and relaxation while reducing or eliminating the need for sedation. Many administrators and clinicians have come to realize music therapy is not only researched-based, but revenue generating. In the following pages, we will explore some of the advancements and opportunities in the area of music therapy and medicine with children.

MEASUREMENT TOOLS

OVER THE PAST THIRTY YEARS, music therapy has grown and thrived in pediatric healthcare settings. The use of live music therapy interventions has helped many children better cope with the unfamiliar, and sometimes frightening, hospital environment. Research has shown music therapy has been very effective in not only decreasing depression and elevating mood, but also decreasing anxiety pre- and post-surgery and reducing pain for various invasive procedures such as surgical treatments and bone marrow aspirations.[12]

As medical costs continue to rise, it is imperative that medical music therapy programs provide the necessary evidence that music therapy (MT) services are cost effective in order to maintain a permanent position within the hospital setting. One of the ways medical music therapists are able to show this is by implementing services that provide three major benefits, which are:

1. Reimbursement
2. Cost Savings
3. Patient Satisfaction

There are many music therapy services that provide at least one or two of these benefits such as the services listed previously. However, in the last 10 years, new music therapy techniques have been researched and developed that provide all three benefits. By implementing the services discussed this monograph, medical music therapy programs are able to thrive easily within the medical environment.

1. **Reimbursement:** Even though the field of music therapy has been around since the early 1950's, the field is still relatively small when compared to other medical professions. Because music therapy does not have its own set of CPT codes (Current Procedural Terminology) to use for billing, music therapists must find existing codes that directly reflect the services being provided. Many music therapists use the same codes that are used by physical, occupational, and speech therapists to bill for services because the goals are similar. Until now, MT's were only being reimbursed for outpatient services by working one-on-one with each insurance company. The music therapy program at Walt Disney Pavilion at Florida Hospital for Children was the first program to find and implement CPT codes that made it possible to bill for inpatient music therapy services in the neonatal intensive care unit.

2. **Cost Savings:** When implementing a music therapy program or any new medical service within the healthcare environment, there are two main areas that administrators look at: mission and margin.

    > The mission is very important and healthcare administrators look at how each service can carry out that mission in its daily responsibilities with patients and staff. The margin, or how each facility will save or make money, is equally important. Many good programs and services are rarely implemented if each is unable to show the cost-effectiveness of service.

    Music therapy provides many services that save a hospital money, from shortening length of stay to decreasing or eliminating certain medications used for common side effects or procedures.

3. **Patient Satisfaction:** Facilities across the country are discovering that patient satisfaction is gaining momentum as one of the primary standards for measuring a healthcare organizations success. It may also be a primary revenue source in healthcare in the future. A movement is under way to link the amount of funding a facility receives from the government to its patient satisfaction scores. This issue has become a primary focus for many healthcare systems along with incorporating new services and programs that boost these scores. Here, music therapy can play an important role. Using patient preferred live music with evidence-based techniques, music therapists can accomplish goals such as decreased pain for a chronic pain patient or help a premature infant tolerate the hospital environment which helps to increase overall patient satisfaction.

The three measurement tools or benefits listed above are critical when implementing a new medical music therapy program or enhancing an existing program.

7 COMMON PEDIATRIC MUSIC THERAPY SERVICES

B ELOW IS A LIST OF PEDIATRIC MUSIC THERAPY SERVICES that are being used in children's hospitals today that contain at least one of the three of the measurement tools previously discussed.

1. **Neonatal Intensive Care Unit:** Music therapy services in the NICU are used with premature infants to increase tolerance to the hospital environment as well as promote non-nutritive sucking for infants who have been diagnosed with "poor oral feeding" skills. Music therapy services can also be used to educate parents on how to interact with their baby properly using music to prevent over-stimulation.

    Because many premature infants experience neurological implications, they have a greater chance of needing special education services for various diagnoses such as learning disabilities, cerebral palsy, mental retardation and hyperactivity. Music therapists who work in a NICU have done specialized research showing that music can help accomplish developmental and medical objectives when used properly. A variety of physiological and behavioral variables have been positively effected by music such as behavior state, heart rate, respiration rate, oxygen saturation level, weight gain, and days in hospital. But there are three primary uses of NICU music therapy that promote growth and development in the premature infant: 1) music to mask aversive environmental stimuli and reduce stress thereby promoting physiological well-being and stability; 2) music to assist neurological maturation and teach tolerance to stimulation; 3) and music to reinforce non-nutritive sucking (Standley & Whipple, 2003).[13]

In 1998, Standley found by using multimodal stimulation paired with live lullaby music, female premature infants were able to tolerate the NICU environment and leave the hospital an average of 11.9 days sooner than those who did not receive music.[14] Shortly after (2003), Standley also found premature infants who had been deemed poor oral feeders could feed at a higher rate using the PAL (Pacifier Activated Lullaby).[15]

NICU music therapy services utilize all three measurement tools and can be vital when implementing or expanding a music therapy program.

> Florida Hospital was the first hospital in the United States to receive reimbursement for inpatient music therapy services in the NICU.

The revenue that is generated each year can fund a full-time music therapist position. Because premature infants receiving music therapy experience a shortened length of stay, non-profit hospitals can experience significant cost savings as well as an increase in patient satisfaction.

2. **Music Therapy Assisted Procedural Support:** There are many non-invasive pediatric procedures which require sedation or general anesthesia in order to be complete successfully such as echocardiograms, computed tomography (CT) scan intravenous (IV) starts and picc line placements, magnetic resonance imaging (MRI) scans, electroencephalogram (EEG) tests, x-rays, extubations and wound debridement. Using patient preferred live music along with specialized music therapy techniques, music therapists are able to decrease anxiety, decrease non-compliant behavior, and use music as a catalyst to begin the sleep process for patients unable to sleep prior to or during a procedure.[16]

Some of the procedures listed above have been proven cost-effective by using live music therapy techniques to eliminate the need for sedation. In 2003, Walworth was able to eliminate sedation for pediatric echocardiograms as well as decrease procedure duration.[17] Music therapists can also use music as a catalyst for sleep for CT scans and electroencephalograms instead of using a sedative. Because most, if not all, parents would like for their children to have music instead of sedation, there is a high level of patient satisfaction when implementing music therapy assisted procedural support services.

Currently at Florida Hospital for Children, we have been approved for CPT code set 96150-96155, which is a set of behavioral/psychosocial codes that can be used for a variety of music therapy services such as procedural support. We are in the process of setting up a protocol to begin charging for music therapy assisted procedural support.

Because there are many procedures being performed on a daily basis with our pediatric patients, the revenue that the hospital would generate from using music therapy could pay for a full-time music therapist.

3. **Pediatric Oncology:** Many healthcare institutions are shifting to a holistic model of healing because they have realized the need for psychosocial interventions, especially with pediatric patients who have been diagnosed with cancer. Untreated psychosocial problems related to a cancer diagnosis can not only result in long-term psychological adjustment, but also can lead to treatment non-compliance and increased symptom distress.[18]

Music therapists who work in the pediatric oncology setting use a variety of live music interventions such as song writing, musical improvisation and playing instruments to help these patients express the emotions related to coping with cancer. Structured music therapy experiences have also resulted in increased levels of behavioral engagement, decreased anxiety, and expression of feelings and emotions relating to illness.[19]

Many of the sessions that music therapists have with pediatric oncology patients focus on coping with the cancer diagnosis and decreasing patient pain. Currently, it is uncertain if there are other medical music therapy programs receiving reimbursement for pediatric oncology services. Because these goals are behavioral in nature, the music therapy team will be implementing the approved behavioral CPT codes in an attempt to pay for these services.

Patient satisfaction is usually high when music therapy is provided to pediatric oncology patients. It provides these patients with an outlet of expression as well as normalizing the hospital environment around them. Many patients are able to write songs that focus on coping with their illness making it easier to express their feelings and emotions.

4. **Pediatric Rehabilitation:** Music therapy with pediatric rehabilitation patients is the use of evidence-based music techniques to improve social, speech and language, physical and cognitive functioning in children with a variety of developmental and physical disabilities. It also helps patients who have suffered traumatic brain injury or paralysis. Each music therapy session is individualized to meet each patient/client's needs. Music therapists can also co-treat with other members of the interdisciplinary team such as the occupational, physical or speech therapist. During treatment, age appropriate songs, activities and instruments are used to help motivate each patient and reinforce the desired behavior, skill or goal.

Because music is processed in both hemispheres of the brain, music can stimulate cognitive functioning as well as improve speech and language skills. In 2005, Kaplan and Steele found that music therapy was successful in significantly improving communication and language skills for patients with autism. It was also found that the use of music therapy was helpful in reaching behavioral and cognitive goals as well.[20] Numerous studies support the use of music in the rehabilitation of upper and lower extremities. In one study, music therapy was proven to be significantly beneficial in improving gait patterns in children with spastic diplegic cerebral palsy.[21]

Parents of pediatric rehabilitation patients prefer music therapy sessions because music can help each child be successful in reaching his/her goals no matter what level of functioning or disability, therefore, patient satisfaction is usually high.

There have been many music therapists who have received reimbursement for their services in the pediatric rehabilitation outpatient setting, either in a clinic or home setting. These music therapists must work one-on-one with individual insurance companies to get approval for reimbursement. The CPT codes that are approved are not specific to music therapy, but provide a close definition of the goal and intervention that each music therapist will be using. The music therapy team at Florida Hospital for Children receives many referrals for pediatric patients who would benefit from rehabilitation music therapy services. Because of the recent reimbursement success in the NICU, the MT team has had the set of behavioral codes listed pre-approved for use with this population and will be implementing them. To date, there has not been a research study or analysis that has given information as to whether these services decrease length of stay; however, since it has been found these services increase motivation and success in rehabilitation patients to reach their goal(s) faster, we can only assume music therapy services help to hasten patient discharge.

5. **Pediatric Emergency Room Services:** The use of music therapy services in the emergency room (ER) can be offered before, during, and after medical services have been provided. Music therapists use live, familiar, patient-preferred music and music interventions to help each child gain control over his/her environment while helping to decrease anxiety. The use of music therapy to decrease anxiety pre-surgery/treatment has been proven very effective. One study that was used with children 3 -10 years old resulted in significant decreases in pre-operative anxiety using live music therapy interventions. Music therapy can also decrease pain during common invasive and non-invasive procedures in the ER.

> In 2008, Barton found the use of live music interventions decreased pain, anxiety, and adverse behaviors in pediatric patients undergoing procedures such as incision and draining, suturing, removing foreign particles from the skin and x-rays.[22] There was also 100% satisfaction with patients and their parents during this study.

Most hospitals find there is an increase in patient and family satisfaction when music therapy services are implemented. The patients are able to relax and adapt to the environment much faster with music therapy. The use of music therapy can yield cost savings for the hospital because these services can decrease the amount of pain medication and analgesic before, during, and after medical treatment for pediatric patients. These services can be reimbursable and the music therapy department at Florida Hospital is planning on implementing the health and behavior CPT codes that were approved to cover these services.

6. **Music Therapy in Pediatric Intensive Care:** Many children admitted to the pediatric intensive care unit endure illness or injury involving one or more of the major body systems. Because of the severity of these medical conditions, children in the critical care unit require mechanical ventilation, which can cause signs of distress such as anxiety, increase in heart rate, and decrease in oxygen saturation. Music therapists can decrease distress by using live music interventions to assist regulation through entrainment of heart rate and respiratory rate, relaxation of muscle tone, and decreased work of breathing, which facilitates overall oxygenation.[23] Music can also help with the psychosocial needs of long-term pediatric patients in the PICU by normalizing the environment, providing an outlet for self-expression and communication, and increasing coping skills.

Music therapy services in the critical care unit for patients on a mechanical ventilator can be cost-effective. For long-term ventilator patients, music therapy can decrease the amount of sedatives and analgesics by helping to keep each patient calm and relaxed. Music therapists can also work with children coming off of the ventilator by providing specific exercises that focus on increasing breath support and vocal volume prior and after extubation as well as decreasing anxiety during extubation. These services can be charged for using the health and behavior codes that have been approved for music therapy through the American Medical Association. Music therapy can also increase patient and family satisfaction in the intensive care unit by proving normal parent and child interaction through specific music activities.

7. **General Pediatrics:** Even though pediatric patients that are admitted into a general pediatric setting do not usually stay for an extended period of time, they still experience similar feelings and emotions that a pediatric oncology or ICU patient may experience. The hospital can be a scary place that is filled with unfamiliar people and objects. Pediatric patients often feel a lack of control, which can lead to adverse or non-compliant behaviors, which may include becoming closed off to staff, family and friends. Music therapy can provide one-on-one and group sessions where children engage in activities that promote self-expression and socialization, education and normalization of the hospital environment and a sense of control through structured music activities. Music therapists can also assist in common bedside procedures like IV starts to decrease anxiety and provide distraction during the procedure.

These services, like the previous services listed, can be reimbursed by using the CPT codes that have been discussed. Music therapy can help increase patient satisfaction rates by normalizing the hospital environment and providing positive experiences for patients and their families.

From time-to-time I am asked which of these services is best. I believe all the services listed above are beneficial in their own way and for many different reasons. However, for the rest of this monograph, I would like to focus on the two services that have been proven to be very cost-effective through evidence-based research: Music therapy services for NICU and procedural support.

MUSIC THERAPY IN THE NICU

A FEW MONTHS AFTER STARTING the NICU music therapy program at Florida Hospital for Children, I received a number of calls from reporters and newspaper columnists requesting interviews. In the process of researching other hospitals' music programs, one reporter went to a local hospital and spoke with a neonatologist. She asked him if they had music therapy in their NICU and the physician replied, "Yes, we have a harpist that plays in our newborn unit."

> A NICU music therapist is more specialized than a regular music therapist – and provides a unique set of clinical services beyond a performance musician such as a harpist. Music therapists who work in the NICU must have additional certification (NICU MT) beyond their MT license, which involves many clinical hours of observation, practice, and research of the effects of music therapy interventions on premature infants.

A NICU music therapist is certified to use specialized techniques to increase an infant's tolerance of the NICU environment and the larger world. As such, a NICU music therapist also knows the best type, volume, and length of music for treating each baby, and is able to educate parents and staff about the effects of over-stimulation, and how using music correctly can decrease risks to each infant's neurological development.

As we think about using music in the NICU, we usually visualize a dark, quiet room with soft lullabies playing in the background. However, the use of music is much deeper and more complex than this and few people realize when music is used in the correct way, it has significant effects and can teach premature infants the reflexes and skills needed to survive.

Due to the fragile nature of the NICU environment, it is highly important that hospital staff consult with a music therapist when considering the implementation of music. Because of the extreme tenderness of the premature infant's hearing development, caution must be taken when using auditory stimuli and all variables such as loudness, duration, and presentation should be taken into account. The American Academy of Pediatrics Committee on Environmental Health recommends that environmental noise levels within the NICU be kept below 55 dB on Scale A (scale used to measure frequency of noise). Because music is acoustically different from noise, it is measured on decibel scale C. In the NICU, all music therapy interventions mentioned in this monograph use music that is played/sung at or below 65 dB Scale C, which is equal to 55 dB on scale A, to prevent negative side effects of the development in pre-term infants' hearing.

HISTORY OF THE PAL SYSTEM

THE SUCK-SWALLOW-BREATHE REFLEX that is needed for an infant to nipple or bottle feed is a requirement that babies must meet in order to leave the hospital. When an unborn fetus is between 12-14 gestational weeks, it will begin to engage in the very first rhythmic behavior – non-nutritive sucking. This simple reflex aids in neurological development by facilitating internally regulated rhythms.[24] Even though they can suck, prior to 34 gestational weeks, the neurological system is too immature to support the suck-swallow-breathe response for oral feeding. Babies born prematurely before or at the beginning of the third trimester are fed by tube and at 34 gestational weeks when the brain has matured, they must learn to feed in the NICU. Very premature infants often experience multiple medical problems, and the related treatments may delay the development of the suck-swallow-breath ability decreasing chances for non-nutritive sucking with a pacifier. Also, the neonatal intensive care environment, although carefully designed to support the development of the premature infant, entails frequent alarms and other sounds that would not be present in the womb during the third trimester of development. These aspects of the NICU can stress or over-stimulate infants. When an infant is over-stimulated, a short pause occurs in his or her neurological development. This pause can lead to more negative effects, such as respiratory distress and lack of motivation, or aversion to feeding typically, which results in weight loss and a longer hospital stay.

Nurses working in the NICU will often start offering bottle or nipple feeds around 34 weeks corrected gestational age. As stated before, since very premature infants often have not learned the coordination of the suck-swallow-breathe reflex, the feeding experience in the NICU can be a stressful one. When the sucking pattern is weak and uncoordinated, the infant may likely experience negative side effects such as a decrease in oxygen saturation, expended energy, and weight loss.[25]

PAL PIONEER

Dr. Jayne Standley has received numerous honors and is a Robert O. Lawton Distinguished Professor of Music at Florida State University with a courtesy appointment to the College of Medicine. She is recognized nationally and internationally for her research in music therapy. Dr. Standley has authored three books, numerous refereed research articles published in medical, music therapy, and special education journals and is the current editor of the *Journal of Music Therapy*.

> The goal of music therapy in the NICU is to enable and equip infants to tolerate their environment and to increase the speed with which they learn to feed. MT treatments used to accomplish these goals are known as the pacifier-activated-lullaby (PAL) system and multimodal stimulation.

Music is effective reinforcement for all ages of individuals and for diverse goals within educational, home, and health settings.[26] Although there is a small amount of research that has observed the effects of contingent music on premature infants feeding behaviors, the findings show that playing background music has elicited positive changes in feeding behaviors. Dr. Jayne Standley, Director of Music Therapy at Florida State University and internationally recognized researcher, conducted a study in 2000 to observe two behaviors in premature infants:

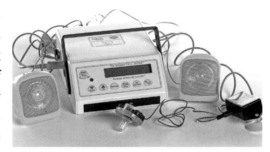

Pacifier-Activated-Lullaby (PAL) Unit

1. She first discovered that the pacifier-activated-lullaby music would reinforce non-nutritive sucking rates of premature infants who were evaluated as being poor feeders.

2. She observed that premature infants could discriminate between silence and music stimuli.

For this study, Standley collaborated with the Center for Music Research at Florida State University to create the PAL (pacifier-activated-lullaby) system. The device used was a Minimam Newborn Orthodontic Pacifier (Ross Laboratories) that was adapted so that a suck of predetermined strength activated an electrical signal to a cassette tape player. Pressure sensitivity and length of music activation could be controlled for each suck. Sensitivity was set at minimal pressure and music duration at 10 seconds with duration reset with each suck. When the music was activated, red lights on the control box were activated which would show sucking frequency and duration. The duration indicator was used for data collection.[27] The music tape for this study included lullabies sung by female vocalists at 65-70 dB and was placed at the feet to the lower side of the infant.

In this initial study, music was played in five-second intervals to see if the infant could discriminate between the music being on and off and if there were any positive effects to the sucking behavior. The results showed an increase in sucking rates 2.43 times greater during music than during silence. This rate decreased significantly after the music stopped and increased again when music restarted. From this study, it was found that infants could learn and discriminate using the music on/off stimuli and there were no signs of over-stimulation during music and silence.

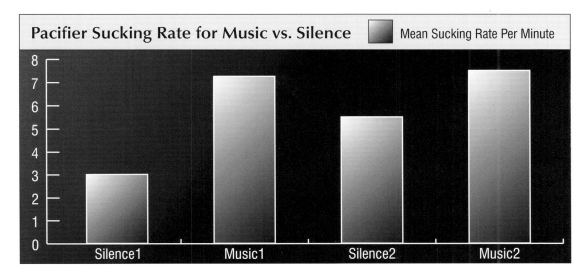

Through non-nutritive sucking (NNS) opportunities, premature infants can learn the oral skills needed for bottle or nipple feeding. Pacifiers given 10 minutes prior to an oral feeding can increase the inactive awake state of the infant and decrease the total length of time for feeding. Infants that need more than 30 minutes to bottle or nipple feed are deemed poor feeders and are given the rest of the nutrition by gavage (tube) feeds to decrease adverse physiological reactions to prolonged feedings. By increasing the endurance and strength of the suck, the nutritional intake increases and the length of feeding decreases, which is a primary goal.

In 2003, Standley conducted another study using the PAL to reinforce NNS of premature infants deemed poor feeders by NICU personnel and demonstrated an improvement in nipple feeding rate.[28] Like the earlier study, the same lullabies sung by female vocalists on a tape player were used. One experimental and one control group were observed for the amount of nutrition that was ingested during a morning nipple feeding with no significant difference between the two groups. In the afternoon, the experimental group was given the PAL treatment for 15-20 minutes, 30-60 minutes prior to the next nipple feeding. The results showed the experimental group displayed a significant increase in feeding rates and the control group remained the same. It was concluded that the PAL helped the infants learn the coordination and skill needed for successful oral feeding. It was also found the PAL helped infants on gavage feedings to transfer more smoothly over to nipple feeds.

The PAL is patented and has FDA approval to teach feeding skills to premature infants. Healing Healthcare Systems of Reno, Nevada licensed the invention from Florida State University and created the first production PAL unit. It consists of a control box that allows for manipulation of music volume, sucking pressure, the amount of sucks needed to cue music, and length of music played. Within the control box, a CD with multiple lullabies sung by children at 65dB is used. A sensor is placed in front of or near the infant in the crib, and is connected to the control box. Two small speakers are placed no less than 6 inches from the baby's ears and plug into the control box. Another sensor that attaches to the back of a Smoothie pacifier (pacifier used for oral stimulation in NICU) is then plugged into the original sensor. If you or your hospital is interested in purchasing the PAL, you should contact Susan Mazer, President of Healing Healthcare Systems.

The use of the PAL at Florida Hospital for Children and other hospitals around the country has proven to be highly successful. The main goals that music therapists have for use of the PAL is to:

- Increase duration of sucking bursts
- Decrease respiratory distress during feeds
- Increase sucking endurance
- Increase feeding rate when bottle feeding or nippling

The PAL can also be administered following painful procedures such as heel sticks and will speed the infant's return to deep sleep more quickly than will a regular pacifier.[29] It can also be given to infants to decrease agitation and increase peaceful state regulation.

One of the first "poor feeders" referred for PAL treatment at Florida Hospital for Children was a baby girl named Amber. Amber was taking at least thirty minutes to bottle feed meaning that because she was not very motivated; her sucking bursts were very short resulting in a prolonged feeding time. Baby Amber could not begin the process for discharge until her feedings improved.

> I came to visit Amber to provide the PAL treatment early one afternoon about an hour before her next feeding. She did well and by the end of the first treatment, she was continuously activating the music with her long sucking bursts.

The next day, I was stopped by Amber's nurse who asked, "Did you use the PAL with baby Amber yesterday?" After telling the nurse I had, she said, "Amber did excellent on her afternoon feed and was moved to the open NICU last night. The PAL worked great!"

Baby Isaac was referred for PAL because he experienced a drastic decrease in his oxygen saturation rate every time he fed or attempted to suck on a pacifier. When I went to administer the PAL, the nurse told me I could try, but if he started to have respiratory problems, I would have to stop. Once I started the PAL treatment, Isaac's oxygen saturation rate shot up to 100%. During the next fifteen minutes of administering the PAL, he did well. The nurse was surprised there was no respiratory distress.

The average number of treatments with PAL at Florida Hospital for Children is usually three times for about 15 minutes each before the baby is feeding well and is discharged.

WHEN MUSIC SHOULD AND SHOULDN'T BE USED WITH INFANTS

ONE DAY WHEN I WAS IN THE NICU, I noticed a mother had put a CD player underneath the crib of her infant, Matthew. As the classical music played, little Matthew kept startling and his hands were held out in a splayed position as if saying, "Please stop!" Even though classical music may be beneficial for newborns, it is not so for the premature infant.

Classical music contains many complex melodies, alerting tones and shifting tempos that can cause the premature infant to experience symptoms of over-stimulation such as startling or crying that can negatively affect the infant's behavioral state causing a delay in the neurological process of development. Some NICUs play classical music overhead through the speaker system in an attempt to provide a soothing environment for the infants. Even though music can help mask some of the sounds in the NICU environment, it is not beneficial and it can be harmful to have continuous background music playing for a room of premature infants. These types of interventions may cause harm and are not recommended.

Another way many parents and healthcare professionals that work with premature infants often think is an effective use of music is placing a CD player or other musical toy in the infant's room to help soothe or relax the infant. This mistaken notion is based on information from makers of various music products for children – not infants. The truth is that while many music products – including classical CDs – may be good for newborns, toddlers and young children, they typically are not good for premature infants. There is also no research showing the effectiveness of these products with premature infants. Just by simply playing music from a CD player or musical toy placed on the crib, the infants I have observed, including Matthew, easily become over-stimulated, which can lead to a delay in neurological development resulting in a longer hospital stay.

> It is extremely important that hospital staff and caregivers consult with a NICU MT to understand how to use music correctly in the NICU environment to help each infant based on his/her own needs and levels of tolerance.

There is a treatment that medical music therapists are doing today to help increase premature infants' tolerance to stimulation in the NICU, while aiding in the neurological development process. This treatment was designed based on research trying to find out the most effective way to use music with premature infants. I receive orders from physicians and nurse practitioners weekly to use multimodal stimulation paired with live lullaby music with their babies because of the proven, significant effects that this intervention creates.

Over the past 30 years, there have been numerous studies showing the significance of using music with premature infants. Some of the research has shown that using auditory stimuli with a regular rhythm helps to pacify infants and regulate respiration.[30] Infants have experienced a reduced length of stay by incorporating music with movement in the isolette and playing lullaby music intermittently each day throughout the NICU stay. Music also affects other physiological factors as well such as oxygen saturation levels and heart rate. Premature infants exposed to music experience a lower heart rate, reduced signs of distress, increased oxygen saturation and a decreased length of stay.[31] Research results also show that premature infants prefer lullaby music over normal environmental sounds of the NICU, radio music, white noise and nature sounds. Using the appropriate style, tempo and volume, lullaby music promotes language development in infants and can be even more effective when paired with the mother's voice. It has been found that infants prefer their mother's voice over any other and respond best to female or children's voices.

There have also been numerous other studies that have shown the effects of skin-to-skin stimulation on premature infants, such as kangaroo care (holding the infant on the mother's chest) and cuddling. Premature infants that receive skin-to-skin stimulation are able to tolerate the NICU environment easier, display organized sleep-wake cyclicity and experience an increase in perceptual-cognitive and motor development. Other studies conducted by occupational therapists found that by administering tactile massages following the cephalocaudal or neurological pattern of development, infants experienced a decreased length of stay.

Using the information from the above studies and results from her own studies, Dr. Jayne Standley created multimodal stimulation paired with live lullaby music to promote neurological development in pre-term infants by increasing their level of tolerance to the NICU environment. In her research, she found that the use of live lullaby music with multimodal stimulation, combining auditory, tactile and vestibular stimulation, significantly decreases length of stay by twelve days for female babies and two days for male babies. In addition, there is a significant increase in weight gain, decrease in heart rate and respiration rate, increase in oxygen saturation, resulting in an increase in overall tolerance for the NICU environment. Other studies were done varying the type of stimulation with and without music to see which was most effective.

All of the results showed that the infants responded best to multimodal stimulation with live lullaby music. NICU music therapists have been using multimodal stimulation for the past several years as a treatment for premature infants. There are over twenty NICU music therapy programs across the country and the number is rapidly growing.

MULTIMODAL STIMULATION TREATMENT

THE MULTIMODAL STIMULATION TREATMENT CONSISTS of three different layers of stimulation: auditory, tactile and vestibular. The goal is to increase tolerance to the daily activities in the NICU environment that the infant controls based on signs of positive and negative stimulation. The treatment is no more than 20 minutes long and involves live lullaby singing paired with a series of massages and rocking for movement. The massage pattern used follows the body's pattern for neurological development: head to feet, message strokes moving from the inside of the body out. The music is sung at a soft decibel and is slow, repetitive, constant and non-alarming which is what the premature infant responds to best. As each layer of stimulation is administered, careful observation of the infant is critical as not to over-stimulate. When the infant displays signs of over-stimulation, the process is stopped until the infant is comfortable again and then the treatment begins again.

Before starting, the music therapist/caregiver must consult with a physician/nurse practitioner to receive a referral or order to make sure each baby is appropriate. Premature infants who are at least 32 weeks adjusted gestational age and exhibit signs of physiological distress such as decreased oxygen saturation levels and high respiration rates are appropriate. Infants with parents that are wary of interaction with their baby or over-stimulating their baby are also appropriate candidates. Multimodal stimulation is also good for infants who have been exposed to drugs in the womb. These babies usually exhibit signs of agitation and distress causing them to be extremely sensitive the NICU environment. Babies on respiratory assistance machines such as a ventilator can be seen; however, they are considered appropriate for treatment on a case-by-case basis.

Once a referral or order is received, a consult with the infant's nurse must be conducted. This is done prior to each treatment to make sure the infant is appropriate. Once determined appropriate, the infant may be taken out of the isolette or crib and held by the MT/caregiver in either a rocker or swivel chair. After the infant is settled, careful attention must be paid to the monitors to make sure all physiological signs, such as the oxygen saturation rate, are stable and the baby is not displaying any signs of over-stimulation such as grimacing, crying, etc., before beginning the therapy. If it is possible, the lights should be dimmed to provide for a more soothing environment.

Auditory Stimulation: The first part of the treatment consists of live lullaby music sung for at least 30 seconds prior to adding other types of stimulation. Because infants prefer the mother's voice over any other, female voices are preferred when singing. Some types of music, such as classical, are not beneficial when working with premature infants. Through years of research, music therapists have found that the type of music premature infants respond to best is lullaby music. The characteristics of this music – slow, repetitive, soft – are the reasons why is works best. This type of music is very soothing because it is predictable and non-alarming. The voice can be used alone or paired with an accompanying instrument such as a guitar.

NICU Music Therapy in Action

When singing, the music must stay at or under 65 dB (C) as mentioned earlier, and maintain a steady, slow tempo at 60 beats per minute. The melodies should be sung in a high vocal range which infants hear best. If an accompanying instrument is going to be used, two music therapists will be needed, one to provide the multimodal stimulation and one to play. Both therapists should sing throughout the duration of the treatment. The accompaniment should be done in a simple, finger picking style. Lullabies that contain 2-4 chord changes and simple melodies work best. An example of this would be "Twinkle, Twinkle Little Star" or "The Wheels on the Bus." The lullabies should be hummed for the first 30 seconds; then singing is added to provide a gradual implementation of auditory stimulation.

When providing multimodal stimulation, it is important to keep track of the positive signs to treatment as well as the negative signs of over-stimulation. Positive signs would be smiling, making eye contact, vocalizing, head orientation to the stimulus or snuggling.

Negative signs of over-stimulation are facial grimace, crying, halt or splay hand, startling, yawning, pulling away from stimulus such as arching the back, tongue protrusion, hiccups, and physiological signs such as decreased oxygen saturation or increased heart rate and respiration rate. When any of the negative signs of over-stimulation are observed, treatment should stop until the baby has reached a level of homeostasis. Once this has occurred, treatment should continue. If negative signs are observed during the first 30 seconds of auditory stimulation, the music should stop and then continue when the infant appears to be comfortable or stable. Once the infant is tolerating auditory stimulation, the next level of tactile stimulation is added.

Tactile Stimulation: Tactile stimulation consists of a series of massages that follow the same pattern as the body during neurological development: head down to feet, inside of body out to limbs. Auditory stimulation should continue as tactile stimulation is added. Each massage should be done in either a linear or a circular pattern depending on the location on the body and should only last 30 seconds at a time.

The following are the massages used in multimodal stimulation:

1. **HEAD** – Use finger to stroke from back of head to front

2. **BACK** – Stroke infant's back from neck down

 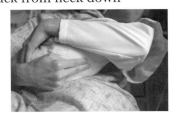 

3. **BACK** – Move finger in circular motion on back

4. THROAT – Stroke both sides of infant's neck, going from back of neck to front
(15 seconds on each side)

5. ARMS – Stroke both arms moving down from shoulder to wrist *(15 seconds each)*

6. ABDOMEN – Stroke abdomen from chest down

7. LEGS – Stroke both legs moving down from hips to ankle *(15 seconds each)*

8. CHEEKS – Using one finger, stroke infant's cheeks, moving from eye down to jaw
(15 seconds each)

9. FOREHEAD – Stroke infant's forehead from left to right side

10. NOSE TO EAR – Stroke both sides of infant's face, moving finger from nose under eye to the ear *(15 seconds each)*

If there are any signs of negative stimulation observed, tactile stimulation should cease until the patient reaches a level of homeostasis. If the infant is still showing signs of over-stimulation, the lullaby music should also stop until the infant is comfortable. Once this has happened, then auditory and tactile stimulation may be gradually added, with tactile stimulation starting at same location in which the infant became over-stimulated. After the infant has tolerated auditory stimulation paired with the entire sequence of tactile stimulation, then the third layer of stimulation is added – vestibular.

Vestibular Stimulation: Vestibular or movement stimulation consists of rocking the infant side-to-side or back and forth, and is concurrent with the tactile and auditory stimulation only after the infant has demonstrated tolerance to tactile and auditory.

> Movement aids in the development of the vestibular system, which controls the sense of movement and balance and is considered to have the most influence on the other sensory systems.

The vestibular system is located in the inner ear and responds to three planes of movement: back and forth, side-to-side, and over the top of the head from right to left shoulder. Development of this sense will help the infant acclimate to movement in space, as well as develop a sense of balance and coordination.

Vestibular stimulation should only be attempted after the infant tolerates auditory and tactile stimulation. The therapist/caregiver can provide this type of stimulation by either rocking in a large back and forth motion or moving side-to-side as if in a swivel chair. The movement must be large and continuous. When this layer of stimulation is added, singing continues and the infant is observed to make sure there are no negative signs of over-stimulation. When the infant has displayed a positive behavioral state, then the tactile process begins all over again starting with the head. At this point, the infant is now receiving three layers of stimulation. As always, if signs of over-stimulation are present, then stimulation ceases until the infant reaches homeostasis. The multimodal treatment should only last 20 minutes. When the treatment is over, each layer of stimulation should be taken away in the reverse order of which it was applied. If the baby made it all the way through tactile progression with movement, then the rocking should slowly come to a stop. The lullaby music should be played/sung for 30 more seconds and then cease.

By implementing auditory, tactile and vestibular stimulation, the premature infant begins to adapt to the NICU environment. While the music helps to mask many of the alarming sounds in the NICU, the tactile and vestibular stimulation helps each infant tolerate being held and touched by staff and parents. The higher the tolerance level is to the environment, the faster the infant will develop, decreasing negative responses to over-stimulation, which may lead to a shortened length of stay in the NICU.

> This treatment also provides for a great bonding experience between the parent and infant. Research has shown that when parents are taught how to perform this treatment, it increases their visitation time in the NICU and they feel empowered to enhance their child's development, while at the same time decreasing chances to over-stimulate and increasing appropriate parent interaction.[32]

AVOIDING OVER STIMULATION

IT IS VERY COMMON FOR MY TEAM AND I to educate parents on how not to over-stimulate their infant. Many parents are scared to hold or even visit their baby because they fear they might cause harm to their newborn.

A few months ago, we received orders for an infant named Jesse who was exposed to drugs in the womb and showed multiple signs of agitation including constant crying. We started seeing little Jesse for multimodal stimulation to help decrease some of the agitation and to slowly start building his tolerance to the NICU environment. When we first started having sessions with Jesse, we just played soft, live lullaby music in small increments while he was lying in his crib. As we progressed to holding Jesse, he eventually became calm during the music stimulation, and we added the tactile and vestibular treatments. During one of our sessions, the parents showed up. They admitted to me that even though they held their son a lot, they did not enjoy it because he cried most of the time. My colleague and I explained the process of multimodal stimulation and then taught them how to do it. We also told them about the negative signs of over-stimulation and what to do if they noticed such signs.

About a week later, the parents told me they felt much more comfortable around their baby and even enjoyed singing and doing the multimodal stimulation. Baby Jesse had a long stay in the NICU because of complex medical problems. He, however, did a great job during music therapy and eventually loved it. Once he was tolerating multimodal stimulation, we began to add other developmental music activities to help him reach his developmental milestones. Multimodal stimulation and music became an important part of baby Jesse's treatment. Not only did it help him to tolerate the stressful NICU environment, it provided him and his parents a more positive experience.

There are some babies referred to us whose mothers gave them up for adoption, therefore there is no family to visit. One such referral was baby Emma. This infant was born very premature and when we started working with her, she was less than three pounds and was in an isolette. The first time we worked with her, she responded quite well. By the second time we treated her, she tolerated almost the entire multimodal progression. In the meantime, a family decided to adopt her. When they first started visiting Emma, I met with them and showed them how to do multimodal stimulation as well as taught them the signs of positive and negative stimulation. By the third visit, baby Emma had reached three pounds and had graduated to an open crib. Her new parents, who were almost always there, thanked me and the team for showing them how to use music with her effectively. Shortly after she had reached three pounds, Emma was ready for discharge. Her family said they would continue the multimodal stimulation and praised the music therapy team for helping them feel more confident when caring for baby Emma.

Baby Nathan was referred to music therapy for multimodal stimulation to help increase his tolerance to stimulation. He had been diagnosed with respiratory distress syndrome and could not breathe on his own. Baby Nathan had been placed on a device called a nasal cannula that delivered supplemental oxygen to his lungs. For an adult, this thin, clear, plastic tubing is placed under the nose and is somewhat uncomfortable. For the premature infant, a nasal cannula can be much more complex to place. It consists of two large tubes that go on both sides of the infant's face and is taped underneath the nose to hold in place. This device can be very over-stimulating to the premature infant.

When we went to see this baby for the first time, the nurse told us he had been crying and was very touchy. I put a gown on and sat down next to his crib while the nurse handed him to me. Baby Nathan was crying the entire time he was being moved, but finally settled down once I was holding him. As he was starting to calm down, I noticed on the monitor he had an abnormally high heart rate. The nurse told me that she would watch the monitor because his heart rate had been known to go above 200, which is too high and dangerous for the infant. My coworker pulled out her guitar and we waited in silence for a few minutes before beginning. His breathing was still fast, but he had calmed down and had stopped crying. I gave the signal for my colleague to start playing.

In the first few seconds of lullaby music, Baby Nathan took in what sounded like a big sigh and started to breathe slower. As I began the multimodal stimulation, his heart rate became stable. Throughout the treatment, Baby Nathan was fine, giving only a few signs of over-stimulation when we were attempting to touch his face probably because of the nasal cannula. The nurse entered the room towards the end of the treatment and couldn't believe how well he was doing. "He looks so relaxed! I'm going to make sure to turn his music box on more often," she said. Before we left, we informed the nurse he was very sensitive on his face. We also were able to educate her on the appropriate length of time and volume for music if she turns his music box on. The treatments that followed went even better, as Baby Nathan allowed us to touch his face during multimodal stimulation and eventually he was able to tolerate the entire treatment without showing signs of over-stimulation.

DECIDING WHETHER NICU MUSIC THERAPY IS RIGHT FOR YOUR FACILITY

TODAY, MANY HOSPITALS ARE MOVING TOWARD a more holistic approach to healthcare, making it an excellent time for music therapists to implement medical music therapy programs. When researching hospitals to determine good places to implement a program, there are a few important points to consider. The first is whether the hospital is a non-for-profit or private facility. This factor can have both positive and negative side effects depending on how the institution is financed.

Music therapy typically works well in a non-for-profit hospital because there is often more room to show how music therapy can be cost-effective. Most non-for-profit hospitals accept patients with or without insurance, which usually means the hospital will lose a lot of money covering healthcare costs for non-insured patients. There are many patient populations in which music therapy services can decrease length of stay and medication, which saves the hospital money.

Typically, a private institution will only accept patients if they are insured, meaning these types of hospitals aren't losing as much money and may not be as focused on reducing expenses through treatments like music therapy. In these cases, it is important to look at reimbursement and how much the hospital will receive from insurance for music therapy services provided. At Florida Hospital for Children, all premature infants in the neonatal intensive care unit whose insurance provider covers these services are charged for music therapy so there is a significant return on investment.

> A healthcare institution's mission statement is something commonly overlooked when trying to start a music therapy program. Yet, it can be a very important piece. Especially if it is a faith-based hospital. Many faith-based healthcare facilities – like Florida Hospital for Children – believe in a mission that centers on whole person care. Music therapy fits well into this type of mission because it is a healthcare field that focuses on healing the mind, body and spirit.

Of course, music therapy can also fit well into non-faith based institutions, but it may be more difficult to show a parallel between music therapy and the hospital's mission statement.

In March 2005, I began contacting various administrators and staff at Florida Hospital to propose implementing a medical music therapy program. I had put a proposal together that included information about music therapy, research and cost-savings. In August 2005, I was able to present to a panel of directors and clinical staff, and two weeks later, the program was started as a pilot program. Within the first year, there were certain goals the program had to achieve in order to be permanently implemented into the hospital system. Along with some small research studies, I discussed implementing a NICU MT program because of the cost-savings as well as the significant effects it has on premature infants. After meeting with various directors, including the medical director for the neonatal intensive care unit, the NICU MT program began just six months after I had begun the medical MT program.

WHO TO CONTACT TO GET STARTED

THE FIRST PERSON TO CONTACT is the medical director of the NICU. This is usually a neonatologist that not only works in the NICU, but decides what services and treatment will be provided. The nurse managers in the NICU should also be contacted along with any speech, occupational and child life specialists. It is also important to contact the healthcare administrators of the facility.

Once everyone has been contacted, materials about the program should be sent that includes information about music therapy; services that would be provided; and possible savings the NICU would experience. It's also important to invite all of these healthcare professionals to the initial presentation. Providing all of the correct educational and research information is vital for making the initial presentation a success.

One important factor to consider when starting a NICU music therapy program is the NICU level and patient volume. There are many hospitals that have excellent women and children services, but do not have a neonatal intensive care unit. When premature infants are born at these facilities, they are usually transported to a healthcare facility that has a level 2 or 3 NICU.

Florida Hospital for Children has a 60-bed, level-3 NICU. This is considered a large NICU and it provides many opportunities for music therapy. At Florida Hospital for Children, music therapy also provides services in level 2 for babies that have reached at least 32 weeks corrected gestational age and have minimal medical problems. Some hospitals have level-2 neonatal intensive care units with only 10 beds.

Even though there are a low number of beds, there are still many opportunities for music therapy treatments and parent education. With the new reimbursement practices available and significant benefits of multimodal stimulation and PAL, the return on investment is beneficial for almost any size NICU.

BARRIERS TO STARTING A NICU
MUSIC THERAPY PROGRAM

WHEN STARTING A NICU MUSIC THERAPY PROGRAM there are a number of barriers you are likely to encounter. Let's look at a few of them and ways to overcome them.

1. **Physicians and clinical staff misunderstand music therapy.** Many people, including healthcare professionals, do not know about the field of medical music therapy. If they are familiar with the concept at all, many believe it is merely a volunteer program where musicians drop by the hospital to play soothing music to calm patients down. It may be nice, they reason, but hardly necessary and certainly not a clinical discipline.

    It is imperative that the medical director, neonatologists, nurse practitioners, nurses, and all other clinical staff associated with the NICU, know the difference between medical music therapy and other alternative therapies. The clinical staffs in the NICU, especially the nurses, are extremely protective of premature infants and must understand that music therapists are highly qualified professionals that use research-based interventions. While there may be some initial reluctance or misunderstanding among the healthcare team, if you are patient, helpful and offer to provide in-service training, in time you will receive good support.

2. **The belief that music therapy isn't scientific.** Many administrators, physicians and nurse practitioners, as well as other staff, will want to see research demonstrating the effectiveness of music therapy services. It is important to know all of the resent research studies and be able to provide this research information to all inquiring staff. In addition, most of the research regarding music therapy in the NICU is quantitative, measuring physiological signs such as oxygen saturation rates and heart rate, as well as weight gain and length of stay in NICU.

3. **The belief that music therapy provides little to no Return on Investment (ROI).** Even if you have hospital administrators and medical staff that like the idea of having a medical music therapy program, many believe they can't justify it because there is little to no Return on Investment. This is not true. A good ROI can be established and an excellent case made for providing medical music therapy services.

NICU music therapy interventions are highly effective and should be a reimbursable service in every hospital. Using music therapy significantly decreases length of stay, which saves the hospital money. At Florida Hospital, music therapy is a reimbursable service and was the first hospital ever to do so. Other hospitals like Tallahassee Memorial Hospital are now also receiving reimbursement for these services. (See Part 3 of this monograph to learn the steps to getting reimbursement for a NICU Music Therapy Program.)

HOW TO MAKE THE NICU MUSIC THERAPY PROGRAM A HUGE SUCCESS

FROM A PATIENT AND FAMILY PERSPECTIVE:

- **Educate families about the MT services that will be provided for their children.** When parents or family members know what services their children are receiving, it helps them feel they are a part of their child's care. Many parents that I have spoken to in the NICU love to learn about the benefits of music therapy. Since music therapy treatments in the NICU are non-invasive, parents are very supportive and extremely happy to have music as a part of their child's treatment plan. When we receive a music therapy order in the NICU, we always leave a form on the patient's crib explaining the music therapy treatment their child is getting along with a contact number for the MT in the event the parent or family member needs more information.

- **Teach parents how to do effective music interventions with their premature infant.** Educating the parents about music therapy is important, but it is just as important to show them how to do some of the interventions. We frequently teach parents in our NICU how to do multimodal stimulation so the treatment can continue when the patient leaves the NICU. We also show the parents how not to over-stimulate their child, signs of over-stimulation and what to do when that happens as well as the positive signs to stimulation. As mentioned earlier, there are many myths about using music with infants, so we educate the parents on the correct use of music, as well as the best type of music for their child. Many parents feel empowered once they learn how to do multimodal stimulation and feel less anxious when holding and interacting with their preemie.

FROM A HOSPITAL / EMPLOYER PERSPECTIVE:

- **Focus on reimbursement and savings:** As will be discussed in Part 3 of this monograph, music therapy services are reimbursable and save on hospital costs. At Florida Hospital for Children, NICU music therapy services alone can save enough money to employ six full-time music therapists. Be sure to work carefully with the team at your healthcare facility on reimbursement and details about savings as much as possible.

- **Conduct Research:** Even though the music therapy research is significant with interventions in the NICU, hospitals and healthcare facilities prefer to have their own data, to confirm the interventions provided at their facility have the same results. At Florida Hospital and Florida Hospital for Children, there is continuous music and medical research in all areas of the hospital, especially the NICU. Moreover, when there are significant research results, the healthcare facility gains respect as a leading center for research.

- **Education and communication for staff:** It is important to keep an open line of communication with the staff about music therapy interventions being provided. At Florida Hospital for Children, the music therapy team provides frequent educational in-services for the nursing staff and physicians in the NICU. Because the staffing turnover rates at hospitals are usually high, more frequent in-services provide updated information giving clinical staff a chance to ask questions. It's also important to follow up with each patient's nurse when treatment is completed so the nurses are aware of how each patient benefited from the music therapy program.

- **Attend interdisciplinary team meetings:** Because music therapy is an interdisciplinary service, the music therapy staff should be apart of the interdisciplinary team meetings. Usually, all clinical staff working in the NICU attends these meetings and provide updates about their services. Music therapy should have the same opportunity. This is another great way to keep staff updated, informed and educated on the services, and any new research taking place. This is also a good chance to meet with the other disciplines working with the patients to discuss various patient needs and gain possible referrals. At Florida Hospital for Children, music therapy works closely with speech, and occupational therapists, and child life specialists to discuss which patients may be best for each service.

CURRENT MUSIC THERAPY REIMBURSEMENT PRACTICES IN THE U.S.

OVER THE PAST FIFTEEN YEARS, insurance companies have begun to recognize the significant results of music therapy and have started including MT services as part of certain benefit packages. Most music therapists work with the insurance companies and the case managers directly, to bill for MT services provided for each patient. Medicaid, Medicare and private insurance companies have all been known to pay for music therapy services with client populations of all ages. Coverage varies for music therapy services from state to state depending upon the insurance coverage and policies for each. Many music therapists who receive reimbursement work for Partial Hospitalization Programs (PHP) or are covered under various insurance waivers and are in private practice.

In order to charge for services, specific CPT or Current Procedural Terminology codes, which are defined by the American Medical Association, need to be identified and approved before implementing music therapy services.

> Because the field of music therapy does not have its own CPT codes recognized by the AMA, music therapists must find codes that directly reflect the service(s) being provided.

For example, the code previously used for multimodal stimulation at Florida Hospital was 97533 – Sensory Integrative Techniques – and is defined as "to enhance sensory processing and promote adaptive responses to environmental demands." Multimodal stimulation was approved because music therapists work with premature infants to increase adaptive responses to the NICU environment. Some codes may define music therapy services closely, however, are unable to be used for billing because there may be a requirement for specific medical staff use meaning music therapy may not be a recognized service. The code used above for multimodal stimulation did not require certain clinicians – i.e. physical therapy, etc., provide the service and therefore, music therapy could bill with this code. Information on CPT codes and requirements can be found in the CPT code handbook, as well as by contacting departments within your medical facility such as finance, revenue management or managed care.

Medicare and Medicaid: Music therapists have been receiving reimbursement from Medicare since 1994, and MT is identified as a reimbursable service under the benefits for Partial Hospitalization Programs. Music therapy services fall under "activity therapy" and must be physician ordered, therapeutic, individualized and goal oriented.

Medicaid coverage varies from state to state providing music therapists with many avenues for reimbursement coverage. Music therapists finding coverage with Medicaid have applied for Medicare provider numbers within their states and others have found coverage through waiver programs. Some of the states currently providing Medicaid coverage for music therapy services are Arizona, Pennsylvania, Minnesota, North Carolina, Indiana and Michigan. [33]

Private Insurance: The American Music Therapy Association now reports that third-party payers are reimbursing over 20% of music therapists. Because of the growing demand of music therapy services, this number is expected to increase significantly over the next 10 years. Private insurance companies such as Blue Cross Blue Shield, Humana, Great West Life, Aetna, Metropolitan, and Provident have reimbursed music therapists on a case-by-case basis. Music therapy is very similar to other treatments like speech and occupational therapy in that there is an individual assessment for each client and if services are found to be necessary, interventions provided are goal-oriented and documented in each client's treatment plan.

Other sources providing reimbursement and financing for MT services are state departments of mental retardation/developmental disabilities, IDEA Part B-related services funds, state departments of mental health, state adoption subsidy programs, private pay, foundations, grants and endowments.

REIMBURSEMENT FOR NICU MUSIC THERAPY SERVICES

NOT LONG AFTER I STARTED THE medical music therapy program at Florida Hospital in Orlando, I implemented music therapy services in the NICU. After meeting with the medical director of the NICU and few other administrators, they suggested I try to get reimbursement for multimodal stimulation and PAL. "Both services are highly effective and should be reimbursed," is what they remarked. I was aware that music therapists were being reimbursed, but on a case-by-case basis only in outpatient settings.

I called the reimbursement committee of the American Music Therapy Association and learned they didn't know of any MT's receiving reimbursement for inpatient services using approved CPT codes for specific interventions, but told me I should set up a meeting with the managed care department at the hospital to discuss possible options, if any. I contacted the directors of that department and provided an in-service about music therapy and its benefits, current MT reimbursement trends in the U.S., and possible CPT codes that could be used for each service. I also provided research and information on NICU music therapy services and why I and other clinical staff at the hospital thought it should be a reimbursable service.

The presentation was a success to say the least! The managed care director was amazed at the significant effects our treatments were providing and decided to go ahead and set up a reimbursement process for NICU music therapy services.

NICU music therapy services are charged as a "physician-supervised service," which means we need an order from a physician or nurse practitioner to provide music therapy treatments with each premature infant. Once the order for multimodal stimulation or PAL is written in the patient's chart, it's then entered into the hospital's electronic charting system that produces a notice to the music therapy daily census. When an order is received into the department, a music therapist is scheduled to provide services within 24 hours. Upon an initial assessment, a treatment plan is created, and thereafter, all progress is documented to obtain the goals specified in the CPT code description.

Multimodal Stimulation: The CPT code approved in the beginning for multimodal stimulation was 97533 – Sensory Integrative Techniques, one-on-one for every 15 minutes. The description for services under this CPT code is to enhance sensory processing and promote adaptive responses to environmental demands, direct patient contact by the provider. The hospital was able to receive reimbursement from this charge; however, after looking at the overall revenue report from the first year, we discovered that Medicaid was not paying for this service because they considered the CPT code being used to be "investigational". Because Medicaid is held as the standard for medical billing practices, many other insurance companies did not recognize this code either. This was a big area of concern due to the fact we want as many of our patients to be covered as possible.

After billing for NICU MT services for about a year, I learned a music therapy team at Tallahassee Memorial Hospital was attempting to start charging for their NICU services, however, they were not approved to use the same code for multimodal stimulation because of the reason listed previously. They, however, did find the CPT code set 96150-96155 that is used for health and behavioral interventions. This code set was previously restricted for use by licensed psychologists only. In 2005, the AMA redefined this code set for use by any clinical service addressing health and behavior goals. A letter from the AMA was sent to the American Music Therapy Association stating that music therapy was a recognized service that could bill for services using this code set. Because these codes are not considered "investigational" and provide specific charges for many of the services we provide in the NICU, I had the code set approved by our reimbursement department. These codes are paired with specific revenue codes to further specify services. For example, 0940 is defined as other therapeutic services. Sometimes, insurers such as Medicaid will provide reimbursement based on the revenue code. Below is a breakdown of each individual CPT code with the accompanying revenue code in the set, and how it is used:

TREATMENT FUNCTION	CPT® CODE	REVENUE CODE	CHARGE PER 15 MINUTES	NICU
Health & Behavior Assessment	96150	0940	$57.00	Day 1 of treatment: behavioral/physiological assessment
Health & Behavior Reassessment	96151	0940	$56.00	Reassessment of goals for NICU patient – pt went for surgery, decline in medical status, etc.
Health Intervention	96152	0940	$54.00	*Multimodal Stimulation:* Charge for two 15 minute units *PAL:* Charge per 15 minutes of treatment following painful procedure
Group Intervention	96153	0940	$12.00	N/A
Behavioral Intervention With Family *(With Patient Present)*	96154	0904	$53.00	Multimodal Stimulation training with family
Behavioral Intervention With Family *(Without Patient Present)*	96155	0940	$55.00	Multimodal training or counseling with family

Listed below are the multimodal stimulation services that are billed, as they relate to the charges above, that our music therapy team provides in the NICU. All services are evidence-based and have been proven effective through research.

- Multimodal Stimulation to promote neurological development to increase tolerance to the NICU environment and shorten length of stay;

- Counseling or training for parents who are anxious about caring for their baby to promote bonding and interaction that is not over-stimulating for the infant;

- Multimodal stimulation training for parents;

- Multimodal stimulation and/or music listening to stabilize symptoms of respiratory distress, increase oxygen saturation levels and shorten length of stay.

As you can see, reimbursement is specific to each individual medical facility. Just because one hospital has approved certain codes for music therapy services, doesn't mean your hospital will follow suit. It is important to understand that each hospital has varying contracts and policies with insurers that will determine the approval of specific CPT codes.

After each NICU music therapy service is administered in the NICU, we log-on to Florida Hospital's electronic charting system and document in the music therapy forms. After documenting, we choose one of the charges listed at the bottom of the form and the charge is automatically entered. The two-page form we used for documentation was created by the Tallahassee Memorial Hospital Music Therapy Department,[34] and is available in Appendix A of this monograph.

PAL (Pacifier Activated Lullaby): The PAL has its own CPT code for billing: 92526, which fall under swallowing/feeding treatment. Unlike multimodal stimulation, this service is billed per session meaning that we charge each time the PAL treatment is administered. PAL therapy charges are comparable to speech therapy services in price and are charged the same way through the Powerchart database at Florida Hospital. The PAL can also be ordered after painful procedures, such as heel sticks, to decrease pain and increase homeostasis. The CPT code used for this came from the health and behavioral code set, code 96152, and was charged per 15 minutes.

RETURN ON INVESTMENT

THE CHART ON THE NEXT PAGE WAS CREATED by Dr. Jayne Standley, mentioned earlier in this monograph, to demonstrate how the revenue received from NICU MT services from the prior year could support a part-time MT position. Prices have been changed to reflect the current charges at Florida Hospital for Children.

The number of multimodal and PAL patients listed above is a conservative number based on a part-time music therapist working in the NICU three hours-a-day, five days-a-week. The assessment and treatment units for multimodal stimulation reflect day one of treatment, while the following two treatment units reflect days two and three. Because PAL is billed per session as mentioned earlier, there is a fee of $181.00 each time. As you may notice, the actual return on investment or ROI of $27,097 is much less than the total charges of $190,251. Because each hospital has different reimbursement rates with insurance companies, the actual ROI will vary at each medical facility. A report we received from our reimbursement department explained that our hospital was being reimbursed at an average rate of 38% for 26% of all multimodal treatments and at 42.6% for 37%

of PAL treatments. As stated earlier, most of the babies that we treated were covered by Medicaid, who didn't recognize the codes that we were using. HMO (Health Maintenance Organizations) and PPO (Private Provider Organizations) insurers covered our services. Medicaid pays a daily per diem rate for each infant, meaning even if they would have reimbursed us for our services, additional revenue wouldn't have been generated. However, the additional costs for services can be reconsidered when the Medicaid daily rate is re-negotiated.

ESTIMATED ANNUAL REVENUE FOR A HALF-TIME NICU-MT IN A 40-BED LEVEL III NICU				
NICU-MT	**TREATMENTS/YR.**	**COST/TREATMENT**	**ANNUAL CHARGES**	**ANNUAL REVENUE @ CURRENT RATE**
Multimodal Stimulation	167 *(Number of infants per year seen for initial evaluation and treatment session)*	1 assessment unit @ $57 + 1 treat unit @ $54 Total session cost = $111 for 167 first visits	$18,537	$1,831*
Multimodal Stimulation	333 *(Total number of second and third visits)*	2 treatment units @ $54 = $108 total sessions cost for 333 visits	$35,964	$3,553*
PAL	750 *(250 infants each seen 3 times)*	$181/treatment	$137,750	$21,712**
Total			**$190,251**	**$27,097**

* 38% reimbursement for 26% of treatments = $5,384
** 42.6% reimbursement for 37% of treatments = $21,712

Reimbursement Issues: One of the issues that arose after implementing reimbursement was that the music therapy program could not receive any of the revenue being returned to the hospital. As the hospital does not receive 100% of the reimbursement charges, instead only receives a percentage of the charges based on the negotiated rates with insurers. Because there are so many services provided to each patient daily, it is too difficult to track the revenue back to each individual service. Nevertheless, by understanding the contracts and reimbursement rates your hospital negotiates with insurers, it is possible to show actual ROI from MT services. In the above table, it is easy to see how a part-time MT could generate more than enough revenue to support his/her position.

Some music therapists I've interviewed have mentioned their hospital would not approve any CPT codes for music therapy services because their contracts with insurers only paid daily rates and MT services would not provide additional revenue. This is definitely true for some hospitals; however, because the literature shows music therapy services decrease length of stay and promote neurological development, there is still a strong case for implementing a NICU MT program, even without reimbursement.

Another reason hospitals may not approve CPT codes for music therapy services is other disciplines within the hospital may be using those codes for their services. It is illegal for two separate disciplines to charge for their services using the same code. When this happens, one of the services will be canceled out meaning one service would not be billed for on that day. You should definitely consult with other disciplines to find out what codes they are using for billing to avoid duplicating service codes. You may also consult your reimbursement department as they are familiar with which codes are already being utilized.

START UP COSTS VS. SAVINGS

THE START UP COSTS FOR A NICU music therapy program depends on specific services the NICU would like to implement. A full-time MT position with benefits, providing only multimodal stimulation is:

Full-Time Music Therapist Salary	$45,000
Benefits	$12,000
Total	**$57,000**

The average salary for a NICU MT in the U.S. is $45,000, and may vary depending on the region where the program is being implemented. A breakdown of average salary by region can be found in the American Music Therapy Association Source book. Benefits also vary depending upon the state and region. In an ideal situation, there are two therapists able to provide the treatment, one that actually does the multimodal stimulation with the patient and the other provides live lullaby music on guitar. However, multimodal can be done with just one therapist singing lullaby music while administering the treatment.

If a NICU would like to implement both multimodal stimulation and PAL treatments, then the PAL device would have to be purchased. Currently, the production of the PAL has been delayed, therefore, the purchasing cost is unknown at this time. If a NICU or any other healthcare facility is interested in purchasing the PAL, they should contact Healing Healthcare Systems in Reno, Nevada, for further information. The size of the NICU will determine how many machines the MT will need.

Due to the significant effects of multimodal stimulation and PAL treatments, the possible savings a facility will incur will typically pay for a MT several times over, depending on how many beds are in the NICU. The national average bed cost of a premature infant is $1200 a day, not including treatments and medication. The number of premature births a year has been steadily rising and is now at 11% of all births in the nation. Because the length of stay is usually quite long, there are many treatments and medication administered, which drive up costs for the facility. Since female babies leave the hospital an average of 12 days sooner with multimodal stimulation, Florida Hospital for Children saved an average of $385,000, due to the estimated decreased length of stay of 29 female infants. The graphs below shows the decrease in length of stay as well as savings vs. costs.

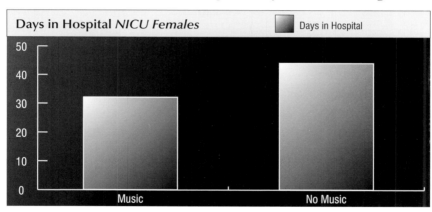

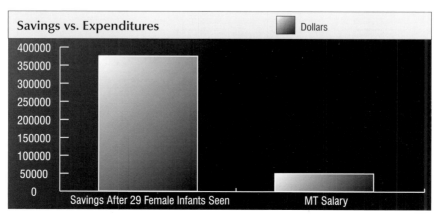

Florida Hospital for Children also receives reimbursement for multimodal stimulation and PAL services. Last year the hospital experienced a return of $5,000 for music therapy services in the NICU. However, our music therapists are in the NICU only part-time. If a full-time position were implemented, the return would be significantly greater due to a greater number of infants treated.

GETTING STARTED: IN-SERVICE, PROTOCOL AND DOCUMENTATION

WHEN MUSIC THERAPY SERVICES are being implemented within a new area of the hospital, providing staff with educational in-services should be done first, especially if the goal of the new service is to eliminate sedation for pediatric procedures.

In-service: Initial contact should be with the director of the department. Provide a thorough presentation of the specific music therapy service you plan to implement. A description of the music therapy techniques for each specific procedure should be explained, along with research and possible cost savings the new service will afford. If the director approves, an educational in-service should then be scheduled for all staff involved.

The in-service should include materials describing the music therapy techniques to be provided along with any research supporting the goals of procedural support. Providing pictures and/or video for visual reinforcement is important in helping the staff understand how music therapy will function before, during and after procedure. Protocol should also be discussed at this time, to inform the staff on how to contact you to schedule music therapy for their patients.

Protocol: It is important to create a specific protocol for each procedure listing detailed information for department staff on when and how to contact the music therapist; as well as a thorough explanation of what will take place when music therapy services are requested. The director of each department using this protocol should be informed first.

At this point, the referral/notification system should be in place, keeping in mind what method(s) works best for the music therapist and staff within each unit. Will the music therapist be paged when a patient is ready for a procedure or will a schedule of patients needing music therapy services be emailed or faxed ahead of time? If music therapy will function as a catalyst for sleep for a procedure like a CT scan, will there be a room set aside for the music therapist to use to help the patient go to sleep? These are all important questions that must be addressed and clarified before implementing MT services.

Documentation: All music therapy services, as well as all procedures provided at Florida Hospital, are documented electronically using the S.O.A.P. format under music therapy in Powerchart, Florida Hospital's electronic documentation system. How the patient responded to music therapy services and if the goal was met, as well as where the procedure took place and staff/family interaction, are all documented. Below is an example of a music therapy progress note with a patient who received music therapy for an echocardiogram:

S: Pt seen in waiting room to build rapport prior to procedure then accompanied pt to procedure room.

O: Pt receiving music therapy for distraction to eliminate sedation for echocardiogram.

A: Pt responded positively to MT aeb (as evidenced by), making eye contact, smiling, singing, and engaging in music therapy activities. Pt sang with MT during procedure and played with a variety of instruments, puppets and other materials. Pt's parent sang with MT and engaged in activities also. Procedure was completed successfully without the use of sedation. Parent and staff thanked MT for coming.

P: MT will return PRN.

A list of all music therapy-assisted pediatric procedures for each patient, as well as the outcome, is kept to measure the overall success for each procedure. This information is then entered into a semi-annual report given to administrators to illustrate effectiveness of MT program.

MUSIC THERAPY-ASSISTED PEDIATRIC PROCEDURES

1.   **Echocardiograms:** An echocardiogram is a non-invasive test that uses sound waves to create a moving picture of the heart. The use of music therapy with echocardiograms has been found to be very successful in eliminating the need for sedation. Before the use of music therapy, children ages 0-5 were given sedation to complete the test, which required an anesthesiologist to administer the medication in a separate room. Because each child was given sedation, a nurse was also required to be present throughout the entire treatment, which could take a total of two hours. After each procedure, the children were taken to a separate room for recovery.

However, when music therapy services are implemented, sedation is eliminated, the procedure time is cut down to 15-30 minutes and an anesthesiologist and nurse are no longer required, significantly reducing costs and freeing up staff, time, and resources that can be used better elsewhere. This also saves space because the room used for administration of sedation and recovery is eliminated.

The process of implementing music therapy services uses distraction techniques, keeping the child's attention on the music and away from the sonographer and camera. When music therapy services are requested, the music therapist meets with the child and parent 10-15 minutes prior to the procedure either in the hospital room, if it is an inpatient procedure, or in a waiting room for outpatient. The music therapist uses live, familiar music and a hello song to build rapport, normalize the environment and decrease anxiety. Once the child seems comfortable, the MT provides education about the procedure in "kid-friendly" terms. If in a waiting room, the music therapist will then escort the patient and family member to the EKG room and help the patient get ready. Throughout the procedure, familiar music and activities are constantly changing to keep the patient's focus on the music. The child and family member participate in the music by playing with small instruments, puppets and other materials that don't interfere with the procedure.

Dr. Darcy Walworth, music therapist and researcher at Florida State University, conducted a comparative analysis study that measured the cost-effectiveness of using music therapy instead of sedation for pediatric echocardiograms. There were 92 patients between the ages of 6 month and 7 years, who received music therapy. The results confirmed that music therapy was 100% successful in eliminating the need for sedation, as well as saving money, time and pediatric staffing resources. Below is a table displaying the cost-effectiveness of using music therapy for pediatric EKG's, created by Dr. Walworth.

The use of music therapy was very cost-effective with a savings of close to $7,000.00 for 92 pediatric echocardiograms. Valuable nursing hours were used elsewhere and the EKG's only took 1/3 of the time meaning that three echocardiograms could be completed with music therapy in the time it takes to do one with sedation.

Brady was a 4-year-old patient who came into the outpatient center to receive an echocardiogram. It was early in the morning when I arrived for his appointment with my guitar and bag of supplies. When I first saw Brady, he was leaning against his mom

COST ANALYSIS FOR ECHOCARDIOGRAMS

Staff / Treatment	Staff Time Per Procedure (Hr)	Cost Per Procedure ($)	Total Cost Per Patient (n=92)
Without Music Therapy			
RN	2	$55.00	
Sonographer	1	$23.00	
Medication	-	$9.45	
			$87.45
With Music Therapy			
RN	0	$0	
Sonographer	1/3	$7.66	
Music Therapist	1/3	$5.55	
Medication	-	$0	
			$13.21
NET SAVINGS			$74.24

Note: Savings per patient = $74.24; total savings for 92 patients = $6,830.00; total RN hours saved for other duties = 184 hr at $27.50/hr = $5,060.00; total sonographer hours saved = 62 hr at $23.00/hr = $1,426.00.[35]

in the waiting room. I walked up to Brady and his mom and introduced myself. I told them that I would be joining them this morning to do some music while the staff was performing the EKG. Brady shook his head "yes" shyly and mom stated "That sounds great!" While we were waiting I began singing hello to Brady and then he chose to sing hello to his mom and then me.

After the hello song, we played some more songs so Brady could shake and play the small maraca he was holding. His face began to soften and a small smile started to appear. Once he seemed comfortable with me, I asked him if he knew what an echocardiogram was and he shook his head. His mom told me that this would be his first time. So I began to tell him everything that would occur. I told him that he would have to lie down and take his shirt off and that the staff would put some slimy gel on the end of the camera and rub it all over his belly. Brady kind of grimaced when I said this and told him that we could play with the gel before the test started so he could feel it. He shook his head "ok" and then I proceeded to tell him that they were going to take pictures of his heart and that he would be able to see and hear his heart on a t.v. screen. His eyed became really wide and he said "really?"

About that time, the EKG tech came out and said that he was ready for Brady. Brady told me he would like to carry his maraca with him and so I sang and played the guitar while Brady shook his maraca all the way to the treatment room. When we got into the room, Brady's mom pulled his shirt off and helped him up on the bed. I could tell by the look on Brady's face that he was beginning to feel a little apprehensive about the exam. The tech said he would be back in a few minutes. While he was gone, I began to explain everything in the room, pointing out the camera and the monitor that would display the picture of his heart. Then I took the gel and put some on my fingers to let him feel it. He touched it and giggled and I assured him that it would not hurt when they put it on his chest and they would wipe it all off when they were done.

When the tech came back, I took my place and the other side of the bed and had all of my instruments and materials ready to go. Once the tech started, I began singing a variety of songs that Brady knew. I played various instruments in front of him as he curiously watched. Every once in a while, he would look at the monitor and we would show him his heart and listen to the rhythm is was making. As the last picture was coming up, the tech needed Brady to lift his chin and look straight up. This is usually a very uncomfortable part of the test because the camera has to be placed at the base of the neck to retrieve the picture. I grabbed a couple of instruments and materials that are interesting to watch and began singing with them above Brady's head.

Brady watched intently as I moved the instruments and other objects around his head. Brady wasn't paying any attention at all to the camera that was right below his chin. "Ok, we're done!" the tech said. Brady smiled as we all cheered at what a great job he did. Brady got down from the bed and gave me a high five. Brady's mom thanked me and said what a great service that was for her son. Later that afternoon, we received a letter from Brady's mom that was sent to the hospital's website praising our team for what a great job we did and how it helped her son relax and have fun.

2. **Computerized Tomography Scan (CT Scan):** A CT scan is a sophisticated x-ray procedure that obtains images of various parts of the body that can't be seen on a standard x-ray. Patients who need a CT scan must lie completely flat for an extended period of time, while the machine takes pictures of specific areas of their body.

Infants and young children who require a CT scan have to be sleep deprived in order to fall asleep and remain still for the procedure. They are also deprived of food in order to have sedation. When music therapy is implemented, music acts as a catalyst for sleep and eliminates the need for sedation making the process quick and easy for the patient and family.

Unlike an echocardiogram, the music therapist uses music to normalize the environment first, and then helps to induce sleep once the patient is comfortable. When music therapy services are requested, the patient must be sleep deprived in order for the music to be most effective. The music therapist will generally meet the patient 30 minutes prior to the procedure and use the iso-principle when first meeting the patient, matching the music to the child's behavioral state and energy level. If the child is anxious or in a very active state, the music therapist may play live, familiar music and activities that might include rhythm instruments and singing to familiar music to help build rapport and normalize the environment. Once the patient is comfortable, the music is gradually decreased to a softer, slower rhythm to help the patient fall asleep. In an ideal music therapy situation, the MT, parents and patient are in a quiet space where the lights can be dimmed or turned off, which helps induce sleep. Once the child begins to relax, the parent is urged to hold his/her child while the music therapist plays live, continuous music on the guitar.

At this point, the patient is wrapped in a warm blanket, which will also be used on the CT scan table. Once the patient has fallen asleep, he/she is transported to the procedure room and then onto the CT scan table. Each patient is different, and depending on the environment and their emotional state, the time varies to induce sleep. However, if the patient is sleep deprived and has positive family support the process generally takes 15 minutes (Walworth, 2003).

While the child is being transported to the procedure room, and throughout the entire procedure, the music therapist continues to play. If the patient should wake up at any time, the familiar music will help the child fall back asleep and the scan can be completed, usually within an hour. Because the patients are not allowed food prior to the scan, infants and smaller children are sometimes unable to fall asleep because of the desire to eat. Parents are given the option to feed their child and proceed with music therapy or have sedation administered. Most parents choose to feed their child and proceed with music therapy with the understanding that the scan will need to be rescheduled if their child is unable to fall asleep. In most cases, the children who are fed fall asleep with music therapy and are able to complete the scan.

> In the same comparative analysis study Walworth (2005) conducted, she also measured the effectiveness of music therapy with CT scans. Out of 56 CT scans performed with children ages 1 month to 9 years, only six were unable to complete the scan without sedation, because they were not sleep deprived. The rest of the children who received music therapy were able to complete the scan successfully without the use of sedation.

Like the echocardiogram, music therapy saves money and time. Patients don't need to be sedated, therefore an anesthesiologist isn't needed. Nurses aren't needed either freeing them to provide more valuable services in other areas of the unit. This is extremely important considering many hospitals are experiencing a nursing shortage. Another benefit is children don't risk side effects of sedation, which can result in a longer stay after the procedure. With music therapy the child and parent can leave as soon as the procedure is complete.

3. **Electroencephalogram (EEG):** An EEG is a recording of the brain's spontaneous electrical activity as recorded by multiple electrodes placed on the scalp over a short period of time, usually 20-40 minutes. Like the CT scan, patients are required to be asleep for this procedure and are usually given a mild sedative to help induce sleep. One aspect of this procedure that causes anxiety is the many electrodes placed all over the scalp. This reaction can cause non-compliant behaviors such as crying and resistant verbalizations. When this happens and the child is unwilling to complete the test, then the EEG will be rescheduled sometimes multiple times until the child can complete it.

The use of music therapy for EEG's makes the process quick and easy for the staff and patient. This procedure is similar to the CT scan; however, a mild sedative is given to the patient to help induce sleep. When patients are unable to relax or have an adverse reaction to the sedative, music therapy is called to decrease anxiety to help the patients eventually fall asleep. Prior to the procedure, the music therapist will meet the patient to establish rapport and give education on why the staff will be applying all of the electrodes to the patient's head. Then the iso-principle is used by using patient preferred music on guitar to match the patient's current anxiety level and then decreased in tempo and volume until the patient is asleep.

One of the nurses who work in our outpatient pediatric unit contacted the music therapy department because an MT was needed for an EEG. When I arrived, the anxious staff member Jason, who was performing the EEG, revealed to me his patient, Michael, who was 7 years old , was about to have his third attempt at completing an EEG. Apparently, the first two times they tried, Michael kept pulling the electrodes off of his head and would not relax. Jason said Michael had agreed to give it another try if music therapy was used. When I walked in the room, I introduced myself to the mother of the patient and then to Michael.

I started out by playing a hello song so we could get to know each other. Michael's eyes fixed on my bag of instruments and he asked if he could hold a small shaker. Shaker in hand, we played a few songs together. When Jason was ready to start applying the electrodes, I told Michael what we were about to do and that he had to remain still, but he could keep play his shaker if he wanted. Michael was happy to keep playing and we sang a few more songs while Jason attached the electrodes to his small head.

Once everything was set, I began singing a song that instructed Michael to take deep breaths. This would encourage sleep and help the sedative begin working. After a few minutes, his eyelids were closed, but he was still listening to me; he slowly moved his shaker back and forth. I slowed and softened the music until I was barely audible. Michael then dropped the shaker and was breathing heavily. Jason informed me he was asleep and thanked me for coming. Michael's mom was very appreciative and amazed at how well the music therapy process helped Michael relax.

Like the procedures listed previously, music therapy saves time and money for electroencephalograms. Because music works quickly to help patients fall asleep, the amount of sedative used is decreased. The time spent trying to get the patient to relax to apply the electrodes is also eliminated decreasing the amount of the overall procedure time. We have found at Florida Hospital for Children, that music therapy is able to induce sleep in an average of 10-15 minutes for EEG's.

4. **MRI:** Magnetic Resonance Imaging (MRI) is a non-invasive medical test that helps physicians diagnose and treat medical conditions. The MRI machine uses a powerful magnetic field, radiofrequency pulses, and a computer to produce detailed pictures of organs, soft tissues, bone and all other internal body structures. The MRI is a large cylinder-shaped tube that's surrounded by a circular magnet. The patient receiving the MRI lies on a movable examination table that slides into the center of the unit.

   The length of time for an MRI is generally 45 minutes, but can be much longer depending on what area of the body is being examined. Patients are required to remain absolutely still while the magnet, which makes loud, repetitive thumping sounds, produces the scans. Because of the nature of this procedure, many patients ask to take breaks if they are claustrophobic or are having a hard time remaining still. A mild sedative can be administered if the patient thinks it will help. Some MRI units have music installed to comfort the patient and help reduce the noise. For pediatric patients, general anesthesia is given so each child will remain still for the duration of the scan.

To date, music therapists have tried using recorded music in an attempt to decrease anxiety and increase relaxation to help patients undergoing MRI scans. Live patient preferred music has been shown to be the most effective in helping to distract pediatric patients as well as induce sleep during procedures such as echocardiograms and CT scans. To attempt to eliminate general anesthesia for an MRI scan, the patient would need to be able to hear the music therapist throughout the entire scan. The problem with this protocol is that a music therapist cannot be in the MRI room during the procedure because the metal in the guitar can negatively affect the scans. It would also be difficult for the patient to hear the music therapist because of the loud sounds the magnet generates when scanning.

> Research is currently underway at Florida Hospital for Children using a new technique created by Dr. Darcy Walworth in an attempt to eliminate general anesthesia for pediatric MRI patients. The technique allows patients to interact with the music therapist the entire time through the headphones used with the existing audio system in the MRI machine. If the research is successful, the goal is to change the standard protocol for pediatric MRI patients to receive music therapy instead of general anesthesia.

5. **IV Starts / Picc Line Placements / Lumbar Punctures:** Using the distraction technique and patient preferred live music, music therapists have been very successful in decreasing the stress that pediatric patients usually experience when undergoing invasive procedures such as IV starts. Malone (1996) found that pediatric patients under the age of 8 undergoing IV starts, venipunctures, heel sticks and injections, displayed significantly less behavioral stress during the procedures than patients who did not receive music therapy.[36] Even though the use of music therapy with other procedures, such as lumbar punctures and a picc line placement is limited, the music team here at Florida Hospital for Children has assisted in many of these procedures and has found the patients and family members experience less stress when live music therapy is provided.

The process of providing music therapy for these types of procedures is very similar to the others discussed so far in that the ideal situation involves the MT meeting the patient prior to the procedure to build rapport and provide any education if needed. Using guitar and patient preferred music, the music therapist normalizes the environment by engaging the patient in a variety of activities that involve small percussive instruments, puppets and other materials during the procedure. Music therapists also use songs that tell a story that prompt the patient to vocalize or breathe. This technique requires the full attention of the patient and is usually successful at keeping the patient's focus on the music and off of the negative stimulus: doctor, staff, needles, etc. By using music therapy for these procedures, there is a decrease or elimination of sedatives. Pediatric patients usually comply better and display less signs of behavioral distress or combative behavior, which means procedures are completed faster, saving time.

6. **Ventilator Extubation:** As previously stated, children who undergo mechanical ventilation often experience anxiety from painful procedures and unfamiliar sights and sounds in the critical care unit. To help maximize the comfort of these patients, nursing staff will often administer sedatives to decrease anxiety and pain. These sedatives, however, can cause adverse affects. Over-sedation may cause patients to become unable to participate in ventilator extubation, which means an increased length of time on the vent. If patients aren't sedated enough, they may feel pain or even agitation or distress that could lead to premature self-extubation.[37] The use of music therapy can help normalize the environment for these patients, as well as decrease anxiety, which can lead to a decrease in the amount of sedative or analgesics given, especially for ventilator extubations.

Music therapists who assist with ventilator extubations use the distraction technique, as well as the iso-principle. In an ideal music therapy situation, the MT will meet with the patient a few days prior to extubation to establish rapport and get a sense of what music the patient prefers. The day of the procedure, the music therapy session is started before the extubation occurs to help decrease any anxiety or stress the patient is experiencing. Using the iso-principle, the MT matches the tempo of the music to the patient's heart rate and respiration rate and will try to decrease it if needed by slowing down the tempo, volume or intensity of the music.

Like the other procedures mentioned previously, live singing with guitar is used. This technique is used throughout the procedure to help the patient stay calm. Once the procedure is over, the music therapist will stay with the patient until they appear to be comfortable and relaxed. Because these patients experience a weakness in regards to breathe support and vocal volume, music therapy services can continue to help increase these goals using specific techniques. Music therapy is a cost-effective service for ventilator extubations because it can decrease the amount of sedative or analgesic needed for patients to stay calm. By keeping patients calm and relaxed with music therapy, the length of time on the ventilator may be shortened and ventilator extubations can be successful on the first try.

7. **Surgical Support:** The use of music therapy interventions with pediatric surgical procedures has been used for over 20 years and is growing in demand in many medical facilities. Even though music therapy has been found to be effective during surgical procedures, it has been shown to have the greatest impact pre- and post-operatively. In a study by Chetta (1981), pediatric patients who received verbal and musical preparation the evening before surgery, as well as music immediately before, during, and after the initial injection of anesthesia, displayed significantly lower levels of anxiety. This was measured by behavioral and pulse rate responses to pain before, during and after injection. The other pediatric group only received verbal and musical preparation the night before surgery and displayed a higher level of anxiety.[38]

Music therapy services are also beneficial for parents and families of surgical patients. If parents are in distress, then it is very likely their children will feel anxious too. By allowing parents and families to interact with their children in a live music therapy session, they are able to gain a sense of control in helping to decrease their child's anxiety. Oggenfuss (2001) found that 95% of parents and guardians reported less anxiety when observing their children participating in a music therapy session prior to surgery and also stated it was beneficial to their children's well being.[39]

Here at Florida Hospital for Children, kids of all ages are seen for music therapy in the outpatient surgery centers. The music therapy department receives an email two days prior to the day of surgery. Music therapists will then go and meet with the patient and family 30 minutes to an hour before the surgery in a preparation area. The materials commonly used for these sessions are a guitar, small percussive instruments, puppets and other visually stimulating objects. The iso-principle is used by matching the music and activities to the child's affect and behavior and then slowly bringing them to a better behavioral state. Many of the children we see are scared and withdrawn when we first arrive. This is usually because the hospital environment is a new and unfamiliar environment with many different people coming around asking questions, wearing masks and working with strange objects and materials. In this situation, the music therapist will approach the child talking softly, and playing soft, lullaby-like music on the guitar. Once the child seems more comfortable, the music therapist might offer an instrument or let the child choose what he/she would like to do. Because most of these children are given a mild sedative when they arrive, they are able to relax quickly with the music and even fall asleep.

Sometimes children become combative or non-compliant when they are scared. Music therapists can use the music to help motivate and even prompt children to complete required tasks like taking medication prior to surgery. We can also sing about people and objects in the hospital that make them scared or provide education about the hospital environment.

Kayla was a cute 6-year-old girl who came to the hospital early one morning for an outpatient surgery. When I arrived, she appeared scared because she was sitting in her mother's lap holding on tightly with her face buried in her mother's chest. When I sat down and pulled out my guitar, Kayla turned her head just enough to see me, but kept her back towards me. I played a soft hello song to her and some other songs that her mom informed were her favorite. I offered Kayla a small shaker for her to play with me and she took it, turning a little more my way. We sang some more songs and she started shaking her shaker more and more and even began to smile.

At that moment, the nurse arrived and told Kayla she needed her to drink some medication. Kayla said "no" and as the nurse kept prompting her, she became more and more frustrated. I then took out one of my puppets and asked her to pick which one was her favorite. She picked the cat and I proceeded to sing a song about the cat and how the cat needed to drink some medication, but Kayla was going to have to drink some of her medication in order to help the cat. I asked her if she thought she could help and she gave a little nod. I sang the song and had her hold the cat while the nurse gave him some medication. Then I prompted Kayla, via the song, it was now her turn and she took a small sip. We sang the song over and over, going back and forth between the cat and her until the medication was gone.

BUDGET AND REIMBURSEMENT FOR
MUSIC THERAPY-PROCEDURAL SUPPORT

SUPPLIES BUDGET: Unlike the costs for a NICU music therapy program, there are more supplies to purchase when implementing a procedural support program. Various percussive instruments as well as puppets and other visually stimulating materials must be purchased. It is important to have a variety of instruments and other supplies for procedures where distraction is a key component, such as echocardiograms. By continuously changing the instrument, activity, and music, the child having the procedure will likely be less drawn to the negative stimulus – needles, camera, etc. Below is a table listing the ideal supplies needed for music therapy-assisted procedural support and can be purchased with a budget of $500.00.

MUSIC THERAPY SUPPLIES FOR PEDIATRIC PROCEDURAL SUPPORT		
Music Therapist Instrument	Guitar	
Pediatric Instruments	Small, colorful shakers Shape drums w/ mallets Lollipop drums w/ mallets Rain stick Kabasa Finger cymbals Ocean drums	Kokiriko Egg chimes Xylophone Egg shakers Finger piano Vibra-tone bell
Visually Stimulating Materials /Other Materials	Expanda-Ball Colorful scarves 3Puppets (should be large and small Books with story that can be sung – i.e. Brown Bear	
Storage And Other Supplies	Large canvas tote or cart on wheels Guitar bag Bins to keep instruments and other materials	

All of the supplies listed above are easy to find and can be purchased at local music stores as well as online. In addition, an office or space to keep the supplies is needed as well as a computer for documentation and music resource needs.

Music Therapist Salary: Based on the 2008 American Music Therapy Sourcebook, the national average for a medical music therapist is $45,000 dollars.*With an addition of $12,000 for benefits, the total would come to $57,000. In addition to an FTE, a budget of $1000.00 should be added for continuing education costs. This includes national and regional conferences as well as workshops and institutes that music therapists can attend to gain continuing education credits.

FTE Salary*:	$45,000
Benefits:	$12,000
Supplies:	$500
CMTE's:	$1,000
Total:	**$58,000**

* This is a national average. Actual salary range is $26,000 – $114,000 for a certified MT working in a children's hospital. The salary may be more if the music therapist has obtained a master's or doctorate degree. The salary will also vary within different geographic regions.

Procedural Support Reimbursement: The music therapy program at Florida Hospital for Children recently approved CPT codes for pediatric procedural support. The codes come from the health and behavioral code set used for multimodal stimulation. Code 96152 – Intervention, has been used in the past by psychologists to provide behavioral techniques such as relaxation and treatment-based education during pediatric procedures. It has also been documented that CPT code 96154 –Intervention for family with patient present, has been used in a procedure setting to provide behavioral services to family members to reduce stress as well as educate them about the procedure their child is going to have.[40] This is very similar to the behavioral interventions that music therapists provide before, during and after pediatric procedures, therefore, these codes were approved.

The process is the same as NICU reimbursement in that the ordering physician or ARNP must write an order for music therapy for the specific procedure. The first procedure using the new codes will be pediatric echocardiograms. Educational in-services have been given by the music therapy team at several staff meetings within the E-KG department, to not only set up protocol, but to inform physicians of the benefits of ordering music therapy instead of sedation. If successful, and the music therapy program expands its services, the same educational format and CPT codes will be used for other procedures discussed, such as CT scans and MRI's.

We don't know the exact reimbursement rate(s) MT services will bring the hospital or how much the return on investment will be because this process has just begun for these procedures. However, because there are so many procedures done on a daily basis that could benefit from music therapy, the revenue earned could possibly cover a part-time or even a full-time music therapy position.

KYLE'S STORY

KYLE WAS A VIBRANT 17-YEAR-OLD BOY. He excelled in school, had a supportive family and big dreams of becoming an architect. One day he began feeling pain in his stomach. Thinking it was just stomach cramps, he took some medicine and didn't think much more about it. In the following days, the pain increased until his mother decided to take him to a doctor. After a number of visits, Kyle was informed he had a rare case of adenocarcinoma, a cancer that invades the epithelial tissue lining the cavities and organs of the body. The cancer was near his pancreas but the doctor seemed hopeful his cancer could be cured.

Kyle was admitted to the hospital and began treatment. Soon after he arrived, I received a music therapy referral for him. When I first met Kyle, he was full of life. Happy, smiling, upbeat. At first, our sessions usually consisted of us singing songs he grew up with and discussing memories of his younger days. Whenever I asked about his illness, he would tell me that he was going to beat it because he had many goals he wanted to accomplish. One day Kyle decided to shave the full, thick, brown hair from his head. The treatments were getting to it anyway he said. When I mentioned his new "style", he laughed and said he had decided to become a "skinhead."

As the weeks went by, Kyle's cancer didn't seem to be letting up and he began to get frustrated then irritated. His parents, who were normally very supportive, were beginning to argue with each other as the stress of Kyle's hospitalization was beginning to wear on them.

> Our light-hearted visits turned into counseling sessions as I tried to help Kyle deal with the reality of his condition. He said he liked the music and always looked forward to my visits because it allowed him to escape from the constant pain while giving him hope that something good would come of all this. The song lyrics we sang allowed Kyle and I to talk about the different emotions he was going through. He said he was afraid but didn't want to talk to his family and friends about it because he knew how emotional they were and he didn't want to make them feel worse.

After three months the doctor's determined the chemo Kyle had been receiving wasn't working well, so they tried other treatments. The cancer was now malignant and had spread to his liver. He became very jaundiced and began experiencing swelling in his stomach and legs. At the same time I noticed how much thinner he was then when we first met.

The sessions with Kyle became more intense as he began to struggle with his own mortality. Slowly he began to realize he might lose his fight with cancer. Seeing this change, I asked Kyle one day if he would like to write a song to get out all of his frustrations, emotions and feelings. Energized by the idea Kyle and I started right away, piecing thoughts and feelings together to create lyrics. I sampled many different melodies and rhythms for him until he heard something he liked.

For a couple of weeks, we worked on his song, honing it to get it just the way he wanted it. Kyle included lyrics that expressed how he was feeling, how much he appreciated his family for being there for him and his hopes for beating the cancer. When we finally finished Kyle's song, I had it printed on nice paper and recorded it on a CD for him. Kyle's family was in the room when I brought the final creation to him. They asked if I would perform the song live and I agreed. As I played and sang, Kyle's family moved closer to his bedside, tearful but proud. When the song was over, Kyle said thank you and told me the song had helped him to express what he couldn't otherwise say. I smiled, nodded, then slipped from the room to give him time alone with his family.

A few weeks later, the doctors informed Kyle and his family they had exhausted all their options. After months of treatment and having tubes coming and going out of almost every part of his body, Kyle said he was tired and wanted to go home. As they wheeled him out of his hospital room, Kyle seemed barely conscious. But as I said good-bye, he reached up to squeeze my hand and managed a weak smile.

A week after discharge, his parents called to say Kyle had passed away peacefully at home. They thanked me for the compassionate care he had received at Florida Hospital and asked if I would be willing to sing "Kyle's Song" at his funeral. I accepted, though I knew it would be difficult. I understood how grateful his family was to still have that piece of Kyle with them.

Music is medicine. It can heal in ways modern science is still seeking to understand. It can open windows of hope to the soul and provide expression to the seemingly inexpressible heart cry. There are many things we don't yet know about the healing effects of music. But we do know it affects patients both young and old physically, mentally, spiritually and socially. And it does so without the potentially negative side effects that can come with so many other forms of treatment.

Is music therapy the cure for all our ills? No. But as research has shown, it is clear that music therapy improves the physiological, emotional, cognitive and social well-being for patients of all ages as well as providing financial benefits for both patient and hospital.

To children in the hospital whose experience may be filled with needle sticks, surgeries and other "frightening" procedures as well as pain, anxiety and a sense of having lost all control, music therapy offers something completely different. Music therapy helps children in the hospital setting by giving them perspective of their situation and helping them feel connected and supported by the hospital staff caring for them.

By implementing a pediatric medical music therapy program, a child with cancer can experience hope through songwriting, a premature infant can be soothed through soft lullabies, and a child undergoing a procedure can sing instead of feeling afraid. Just a few of the many reasons that music is good medicine.

KYLE'S SONG

Invisible, that's what I used to be
Untouchable for this life in front of me
Slippin' in and out of each and every day
This darkness creeping in, it's getting in my way
What is happening to me? Does anyone have a cure?
Can anyone part the sea?

Chorus:

Is anyone out there, tell me who you are
I want a second chance; I'm going to beat the odds
God if you're up there, jump in any time
I want to make it right and leave this darkness behind

The ceiling falls and regret seeps in
I'm upside down; Let the sacrifice begin
My eyes open more, now what do I say

She has my heart, she's my everything
I hope they know how much I appreciate
Every little moment, every little thing

Bridge

Don't feel bad, I'm not a hopeless case
This is just another darkness I must face

Chorus:

Is anyone out there, tell me who you are
I want a second chance; I'm going to beat the odds
God if you're up there, jump in any time
I want to make it right and leave this darkness behind

ACKNOWLEDGEMENTS

THERE ARE MANY PEOPLE I WOULD LIKE TO THANK who contribute to our continued success in the pediatric and NICU music therapy program at Florida Hospital for Children. I am deeply indebted to Dr. Eduardo Lugo and all of the neonatologists, nurse practitioners, nurses, speech therapists, occupational therapists and child life specialists who have been very supportive of our program and have allowed us to have a place among the NICU and pediatric clinical service lines.

I would like to thank Danny Myers and the managed care department at Florida Hospital for seeing the true value of NICU music therapy and making Florida Hospital the first ever to implement reimbursement for NICU MT services. I am also indebted to Des Cummings, Jay Perez, Greg Ellis and all my Mission & Ministry team for providing support and continuing opportunities to present the benefits of music therapy.

I would like to especially thank Todd Chobotar for all of his valuable help and guidance in order to make this monograph possible. I am forever grateful for his understanding, willingness and motivation to promote our program and the field of music therapy. I am also very grateful to Lillian Boyd, Stephanie Rick and Sarah Hayhoe on the Florida Hospital Publishing team for their incredible support and hard work to bring this monograph to life. Also to Spencer Freeman – thanks for the wonderful pictures.

I am truly indebted to Dr. Jayne Standley for her research and study in pioneering the field of NICU music therapy and for her continuous guidance and support. I would also like to thank Dr. Darcy Walworth for her research and advancements in pediatric and NICU music therapy. Her advice and support have been invaluable to me. I am grateful for the knowledge and guidance of Judy Nguyen and Jennifer Peyton for molding me into the music therapist I am today. I would also like to thank all of the music therapy staff at Tallahassee Memorial Hospital and faculty at Florida State University for their partnership with our music therapy team.

I am very grateful and indebted to my music therapy staff and all interns who have provided many hours of hard work and dedication for a successful music therapy program. You are always an inspiration.

I would like to thank my family for their continuous support and motivation in helping me to achieve all of my dreams. I would not be where I am today without you.

Lastly, I would like to thank all of the parents and caregivers of infants and children in the neonatal intensive care and pediatric units at the Walt Disney Pavilion at Florida Hospital for Children. Thank you for allowing music therapy to make a difference in your child's life. And to Marla Silliman and Tim Burrill, thanks for your wisdom and leadership in guiding such a remarkable enterprise.

APPENDIX A:
NICU MUSIC THERAPY DOCUMENTATION FORM
NICU MUSIC THERAPY PROGRESS NOTE

Music Therapy services were:
☐ Agreed to by RN   ☐ Not appropriate at this time,   ☐ Other: _____

Current CGA: _____weeks   Weight: _____ lbs _____ oz; _____kg

☐ Initial Music Therapy Assessment Conducted (see results in Interdisciplinary Plan of Care)

Status Upon Arrival
☐ Patient was lying in crib,   ☐ Lying in isolette,   ☐ Other: _____

Others present: family member, cuddler, staff: _____ , Other: _____

Initial Behavioral State
Active/Awake, Quiet/Awake, Active/Sleep, Quiet/Sleep, Other: _____

Treatment Objectives

☐ Decrease Pain

☐ Decrease Respiratory Distress

☐ Increase Parent/Infant Bonding

☐ Increase Relaxation

☐ Increase Sucking Strength/Endurance/Pacing/Motivation

☐ Increase Tolerance to Multimodal Stimulation

☐ Provide Parent Training in Multimodal Stimulation

☐ Other: _____

Music Therapy Interventions

☐ Auditory Stimulation

☐ Continuous Music

☐ Non-Nutritive Sucking Device

☐ Other: _____

☐ Tactile Stimulation

☐ Vestibular Stimulation

☐ Visual Stimulation

PATIENT RESPONSE

Stimulation Tolerated Auditory and Tactile

☐ Scalp

☐ Back – Linear

☐ Back – Circular

☐ Throat

☐ Arms

☐ Abdomen/Linea Alba

☐ Legs

☐ Cheeks

☐ Forehead

☐ Nose to Ear

Auditory, Tactile, and Vestibular

☐ Scalp

☐ Back – Linear

☐ Back – Circular

☐ Throat

☐ Arms

☐ Abdomen/Linea Alba

☐ Legs

☐ Cheeks

☐ Forehead

☐ Nose to Ear

Positive Responses

☐ Head Orientation
☐ Eye Contact
☐ Smiling
☐ Vocalization
☐ Snuggling

Signs of Over-Stimulation

☐ Halt Hand
☐ Grimace/Red Face
☐ Finger Splay
☐ Crying
☐ Startle Reflex
☐ Hiccups
☐ Arched Back
☐ Tongue Protrusion
☐ Other: _____

Physiological Responses

Initial Heart Rate: _____ beats per min.
Average Heart Rate During MT: _____ beats per min.
Ending Heart Rate: _____ beats per min.

Initial Oxygen Saturation: _____ %
Average Oxygen Saturation During MT: _____ %
Ending Oxygen Saturation: _____ %

Initial Respiration: _____ beats per min.
Average Respiration During MT: _____ beats per min.
Ending Respiration: _____ beats per min.

Responses to Non-Nutritive Sucking Device (PAL)

Start Time: _____   Stop Time: _____   Music Continuous: _____ min
Triggers: _____   Threshold: _____   Music Duration: _____

Initial Sucks/Burst: _____   Pause Time: _____
Ending Sucks/Burst: _____   Pause Time: _____

Prompting: Mid, Mod, Max   Time Until Independent: _____

Previous Feeding Time: _____   cc: min: _____   Type: NG, PO, Other: _____

Comments _____
_____
_____
_____

Plan of Care

MT-BC/MTI will: Attempt to return to address above goals, return PRN, discharge patient from MT services.

Signature   **Date**   **Duration**
_____

NOTES

1   Zimmerman, L., Pierson, M., & Marker, J. (1988). Effects of music on patient anxiety in coronary care units. *Heart & Lung, 17*(5), 560 – 566.

2   Davis, C. (1992). The effects of music and basic relaxation instruction on pain and anxiety of women undergoing in-office gynecological procedures. *Journal of Music Therapy, 29*(4), 202-216.

3   Steelman, V. M. (1990). Intraoperative music therapy. *AORN Journal, 52,*(5), 1026-1034.

4   Standley J. & Moore, R. (1993, April). *The effect of music vs. mother's voice on NBICU infants' oxygen saturation levels and frequency of bradycardia/apnea episodes.* Paper presented at Tenth National Symposium, Research in Music Behavior, Tuscaloosa, AL.

5   Miluk-Kolasa, B., Obminski, Z., Stupnicki, R., & Golec, L. (1994). Effects of music treatment on salivary cortisol in patients exposed to pre-surgical stress. *Experimental and Clinical Endocrinology, 102,* 118-120.

6   Whisnant, R. (2003). Soothing sounds – Music therapy can be used during surgery to reduce pain, anxiety, and even the level of anesthesia needed. *Minnesota Medicine, 86*(2), 38-40.

7   Cermak, A. (2005). *The effect of music therapy and songwriting on anxiety/depression and quality of life in cancer patients and their families as measured by self-rapport.* Unpublished master's thesis, The Florida State University, Tallahassee.

8   Bolwerk, C. A. (1990). Effects of relaxing music on state anxiety in myocardial infarction patients. *Critical Care Nursing, 13*(2), 63-72.

9   Aldridge, K. (1993). The use of music to relieve pre-operational anxiety in children attending day surgery. *The Australian Journal of Music Therapy, 4,* 19-35.

10 Walworth, D. (2005). Procedural Support Music Therapy in the Healthcare Setting: A Cost-Effectiveness Analysis. *Journal of Pediatric Nursing, 20*(4), 276-284.

11 Standley, J. (1998). The effect of music and multimodal stimulation on physiologic and developmental responses of premature infants in neonatal intensive care. *Pediatric Nursing, 24* (6), 532-538

12 Standley, J. M. and Whipple, J (2003). *Music Therapy with Pediatric Patients: A Meta Analysis.* Music Therapy in Pediatric Healthcare: Research and Evidence Based Practice. *The American Music Therapy Association,* Silver Spring, MD.

13 Standley, J and Whipple, J (2003). Music Therapy for Premature Infants in the Neonatal Intensive Care Unit: Health and Developmental Benefits. In S.L. Robb (Eds.), *Music Therapy in Pediatric Healthcare: Research and Evidence Based Practice* (pp. 19-30) Silver Spring, MD: The American Music Therapy Association.

14 Standley, J. (1998). The effect of music and multimodal stimulation on physiologic and developmental responses of premature infants in neonatal intensive care. *Pediatric Nursing, 24* (6), 532-538.

15 Standley, J (2003). The effect of music-reinforced non-nutritive sucking on feeding rate of premature infants. *Journal of Pediatric Nursing, 18*(3), 169-173.

16 Walworth, D. (2003). Procedural Support: Music Therapy Assisted CT, EKG, EEG, X-ray, IV, Ventilator, and Emergency Services. In S.L. Robb (Ed.), *Music Therapy in Pediatric Healthcare: Research and Evidence Based Practice* (pp. 137-146) Silver Spring, MD: The American Music Therapy Association.

17 Walworth, D. (2005). Procedural Support Music Therapy in the Healthcare Setting: A Cost-Effectiveness Analysis. *Journal of Pediatric Nursing, 20*(4), 276-284.

18 Roarke, M. T., Stuber, M. L., Hobbie, W.L., & Kazak, A. E. (1999). Posttraumatic stress disorder: Understanding the psychosocial impact of surviving childhood cancer into young adulthood. *Journal of Pediatric Oncology Nursing, 16,* 126 – 135.

19 Robb, S. L. (2003). Designing music therapy interventions for hospitalized children and Adolescents using a contextual support model of music therapy. *Music Therapy Perspectives, 21,* 27-24.

20 Kaplan, R.S. & Steele A.L. (2005). An analysis of music therapy program goals and outcomes for clients With diagnoses on the autism spectrum. *Journal of Music Therapy, 42*(1), 2-19.

21 Thaut, M. H., Miller R. A., & Schauer, L. M. (1998). Multiple synchronizations strategies in rhythmic sensorimotor tasks: Phase versus period adaptation. *Biological Cybernetics, 79,* 241-250.

22 Barton, S. (2008). *The effect of music on pediatric anxiety and pain during medical procedures in the main hospital or the emergency department.* Unpublished master's thesis, The Florida State University, Tallahassee.

23 Stouffer, J & Shirk, B. (2003). Critical Care: Clinical Applications of Music for Children on Mechanical Ventilation. In S.L. Robb (Ed.), *Music Therapy in Pediatric Healthcare: Research and Evidence Based Practice* (pp. 49-80) Silver Spring, MD: The American Music Therapy Association.

24 Goff, D.M. (1985). The effects of nonnutritive sucking on state regulation in preterm infants. *Dissertation Abstracts International, 46* (8-B), 2835.

25 Hill, A. (1992). Preliminary findings: A maximum oral feeding time for premature infants, the Relationship to physiological indicators. *Maternal-Child Nursing Journal, 14,* 69-90.

26 Standley, J. M. (1996). A meta-analysis on the effects of music as reinforcement for education/ therapy objectives. *Journal of Research in Music Education, 44* (2), 105-133.

27 Standley, J. M. (2003). *Music Therapy with Premature Infants: Research and Developmental Interventions.* The American Music Therapy Association, Inc., Silver Spring, MD.

28 Standley, J. M. (2003). The effect of music-reinforced non-nutritive sucking on feeding rate of premature infants. *Journal of Pediatric Nursing, 18*(3), 169-173.

29 Whipple, J. (2008). The effect of music-reinforced nonnutritive sucking on state of pre-term, low birthweight infants experiencing heelstick. *Journal of Music Therapy, 45*(3), 227-272.

30 Standley, J. M. (2003). *Music Therapy with Premature Infants: Research and Developmental Interventions.* The American Music Therapy Association, Inc., Silver Spring, MD.

31 Coleman, J. M., Pratt, R. R., Stoddard, R. A., Gerstmann, D. R., & Abel, H. (1997). The effects of the male and female singing and speaking voices on selected physiological and behavioral measures of premature infants in the intensive care unit. *International Journal of Arts Medicine, 5*(2), 4-11.

32 Whipple, J. (2000). The effect of parent training in music and multimodal stimulation on parent-neonate Interactions in the Neonatal intensive Care Unit. *Journal of Music Therapy, 37*(4), 250-268.

33 Simpson, J. and Burns, D.S. (2004). *Music Therapy Reimbursement:* Best Practices and Procedures. The American Music Therapy Association, Silver Spring, MD, 62-63.

34 Tallahassee Memorial Healthcare/ Florida State University Music Therapy (2009). NICU MT Progress Note. Tallahassee, FL: Author.

35 Walworth, D. (2005). Procedural Support Music Therapy in the Healthcare Setting: *A Cost-Effectiveness Analysis. The Journal of Pediatric Nursing, 20* (4), 276-284.

36 Malone, A. B. (1996). The effects of live music on the distress of pediatric patients receiving intravenous starts, venipunctures, injections and heel sticks. *Journal of Music Therapy,33*(1),19-33.

37 Stouffer, J.W. & Shirk, B. (2003). Critical Care: Clinical Applications of Music for Children on Mechanical Ventilation. In S.L. Robb (Ed.), *Music Therapy in Pediatric. Healthcare: Research and Evidence Based Practice* (pp. 137-146) Silver Spring, MD: The American Music Therapy Association.

38 Chetta, H. D. (1981). The effect of music and desensitization on preoperative anxiety in children. *Journal of Music Therapy, 18*(2), 74-87.

39 Oggenfuss, J. W. (2001). *Pediatric surgery patients and parent anxiety: Can live music therapy effectively reduce stress and anxiety levels while waiting to go to surgery?* Unpublished master's thesis, The Florida State University, Tallahassee.

40 Noll, R.B., & Fischer, B.A. (2004). Commentary. Health and behavior CPT codes: An opportunity to revolutionize reimbursement in pediatric psychology. *Journal of Pediatric Psychology,* 29(7), 571-578. http://jpepsy.oxfordjournals.org/cgi/content/full/29/7/571

ABOUT THE AUTHOR

AMY ROBERTSON grew up surrounded by music. Whether it was her grandfather singing to her with guitar, going to polka halls with family or singing and dancing to the radio – Amy loved music. She attended Oklahoma City University to pursue a music degree in flute performance. After receiving her bachelor's degree, Amy attended Florida State University where she received her master's degree in music therapy and completed her internship at Tallahassee Memorial Hospital.

Upon graduation she set her sights on starting a new medical music therapy program at the largest admitting hospital in America – Florida Hospital. Though Florida Hospital served over 1 million patients a year, it had no music therapy program.

By developing an original proposal and business plan Amy won over hospital administration and clinical staff. The music therapy program she began at Florida Hospital now covers multiple patient populations including: cardiac, oncology, pulmonary, stroke, pediatric, behavioral health, NICU, Parkinson's, traumatic brain injury, palliative care, bereavement, and physical rehab. In addition, Amy leads drum circles and teaches musical lifestyle enhancement to management groups.

Under Amy's leadership, Florida Hospital became the first in the nation to receive reimbursement for music therapy inpatient services in the NICU. Because of the partnership with Florida State University, Florida Hospital for Children hosts the National Institute for Infant & Child Medical Music Therapy which has been recognized both nationally and internationally with groups coming from as far as Japan, New Zealand and Spain to observe Amy's program and learn about NICU and pediatric techniques.

Amy is the author of two monographs entitled *Music, Medicine & Miracles* and *The Music Therapy Revolution*, as well as several journal articles on her research. At present, she is working on a book for general audiences about the healing power of music.

Amy currently serves as supervisor for the medical music therapy program at Florida Hospital where she continues to practice, teach, consult, speak, publish and conduct original research. She also serves as the clinical training supervisor for medical music therapy interns from all over America.

ABOUT FLORIDA HOSPITAL FOR CHILDREN

Florida Hospital for Children

For more than a century, Florida Hospital has been recognized as a global pacesetter for excellence in health care. Known for its whole-person care approach, *Florida Hospital for Children* has established its own legacy for excellence in pediatric care by its expansive network of comprehensive programs and pediatric sub-specialists. As this community's needs change, *Florida Hospital for Children* has united with Walt Disney World Resort and Disney Worldwide Outreach to create a new and innovative approach to children's health care. Building on Florida Hospital's strong foundation of providing the highest-quality medical services, innovative technology and network of pediatric specialists, this children's hospital of the future will incorporate Disney's expertise in developing the ultimate "experience" through environment and personal interactions.

FLORIDA HOSPITAL FOR CHILDREN
601 E. Rollins Street, Orlando, FL 32803
www.FloridaHospitalForChildren.com
407-303-KIDS

HOSPITAL FAST FACTS INCLUDE:

- **RENOWNED PEDIATRIC SURGERY**. Performing more minimally invasive surgeries than any other hospital in the area. More than 200 Neurosurgeries and Neuromedical procedures performed.

- **WIDE-RANGING SUB-SPECIALISTS**. A team of 70 highly trained pediatric sub-specialists covering 30 pediatric sub-specialties.

- **EXCEPTIONAL EMERGENCY CARE**. Treating 73,000 kids in the Emergency Department and another 1,200 in our Neonatal Intensive Care Unit (NICU) annually. 24-hour Children's Emergency Center staffed around the clock by a board-certified pediatric emergency physician.

- **SURGICAL EXPERTS**. Performing more than 25,000 outpatient surgeries/procedures and another 8,000 inpatient procedures each year.

- **THE KID CAPITAL**. Treating one out of every two children in Central Florida the "kid capital of the world".

- **THE BABY PLACE**. Delivering nearly 10,000 babies annually.

- **NICU SPECIALISTS**. 81-bed Neonatal Intensive Care Unit (NICU) with private family-centered rooms.

- **PEDIATRIC IMAGING**. Services include PET, 3D imaging, MRI and 64 slice CT.

- **PEDIATRIC ONCOLOGY**. A program that engages heavily in research and clinical trials.

- **CHILD LIFE TEAM**. Specially trained therapists known as the Child Life Team who help children cope with their hospitalization through education and play.

- **STARBRIGHT CONNECTION**. An internet-based program called Starbright that connects children in hospitals throughout the country, including playrooms, teen lounges, sibling support, pet therapy, special events and guest visits.

FLORIDA HOSPITAL

The skill to heal. The spirit to care.

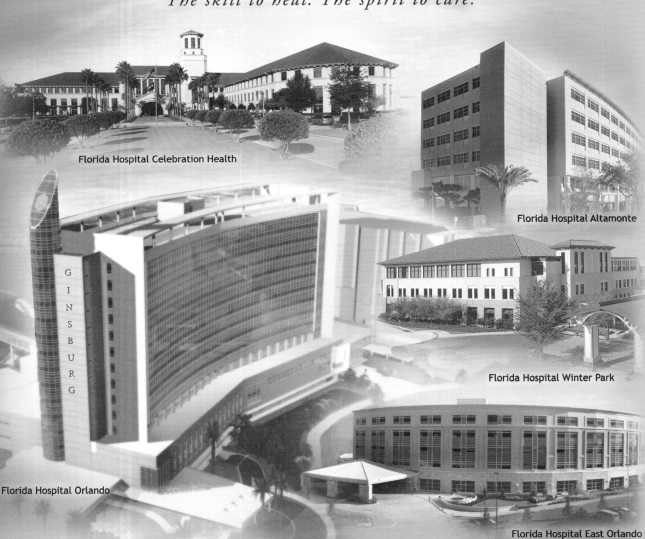

Florida Hospital Celebration Health

Florida Hospital Altamonte

GINSBURG

Florida Hospital Winter Park

Florida Hospital Orlando

Florida Hospital East Orlando

Florida Hospital Apopka

Florida Hospital Kissimmee

ABOUT FLORIDA HOSPITAL

For over one hundred years the mission of Florida Hospital has been: *To extend the health and healing ministry of Christ*. Opened in 1908, Florida Hospital is comprised of seven hospital campuses housing over 2,000 beds and eighteen walk-in medical centers. With over 16,000 employees—including 2,000 doctors and 4,000 nurses—Florida Hospital serves the residents and guests of Orlando, the No. 1 tourist destination in the world. Florida Hospital cares for over one million patients a year. Florida Hospital is a Christian, faith-based hospital that believes in providing Whole Person Care to all patients – mind, body and spirit. Hospital fast facts include:

- **LARGEST ADMITTING HOSPITAL IN AMERICA**. Ranked No. 1 in the nation for inpatient admissions by the *American Hospital Association*.

- **AMERICA'S HEART HOSPITAL**. Ranked No. 1 in the nation for number of heart procedures performed each year, averaging 15,000 cases annually. MSNBC named Florida Hospital "America's Heart Hospital" for being the No. 1 hospital fighting America's No. 1 killer—heart disease.

- **HOSPITAL OF THE FUTURE**. At the turn of the century, the *Wall Street Journal* named Florida Hospital the "Hospital of the Future".

- **ONE OF AMERICA'S BEST HOSPITALS**. Recognized by *U.S. News & World Report* as "One of America's Best Hospitals" for ten years. Clinical specialties recognized have included: Cardiology, Orthopaedics, Neurology & Neurosurgery, Urology, Gynecology, Digestive Disorders, Hormonal Disorders, Kidney Disease, Ear, Nose & Throat and Endocrinology.

- **LEADER IN SENIOR CARE**. Florida Hospital serves the largest number of seniors in America through Medicare with a goal for each patient to experience a "Century of Health" by living to a healthy hundred.

- **TOP BIRTHING CENTER**. *Fit Pregnancy* magazine named Florida Hospital one of the "Top 10 Best Places in the Country to have a Baby". As a result, *The Discovery Health Channel* struck a three-year production deal with Florida Hospital to host a live broadcast called "Birth Day Live". Florida Hospital annually delivers over 9,000 babies.

- **CORPORATE ALLIANCES**. Florida Hospital maintains corporate alliance relationships with a select group of Fortune 500 companies including Disney, Nike, Johnson & Johnson, Philips, AGFA, and Stryker.

- **DISNEY PARTNERSHIP**. Florida Hospital is the Central Florida health & wellness resource of the *Walt Disney World* ® Resort. Florida Hospital also partnered with Disney to build the ground breaking health and wellness facility called Florida Hospital Celebration Health located in Disney's town of Celebration, Florida. Disney and Florida Hospital recently partnered to build a new state-of-the-art Children's Hospital.

- **HOSPITAL OF THE 21ST CENTURY**. Florida Hospital Celebration Health was awarded the *Premier Patient Services Innovator Award* as "The Model for Healthcare Delivery in the 21st Century".

- **SPORTS EXPERTS**. Florida Hospital is the official hospital of the Orlando *Magic* NBA basketball team. In addition, Florida Hospital has an enduring track record of providing exclusive medical care to many sports organizations. These organizations have included: Disney's Wide World of Sports, Walt Disney World's Marathon Weekend, the Capital One Bowl, and University of Central Florida Athletics. Florida Hospital has also provided comprehensive healthcare services for the World Cup and Olympics.

- **PRINT RECOGNITION**. *Self* magazine named Florida Hospital one of America's "Top 10 Hospitals for Women". *Modern Healthcare* magazine proclaimed it one of America's best hospitals for cardiac care.

- **CONSUMER CHOICE AWARD WINNER**. Florida Hospital has received the Consumer Choice Award from the *National Research Corporation* every year from 1996 to the present.

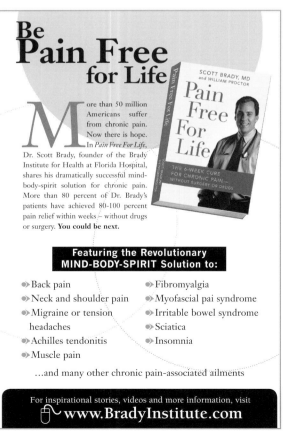

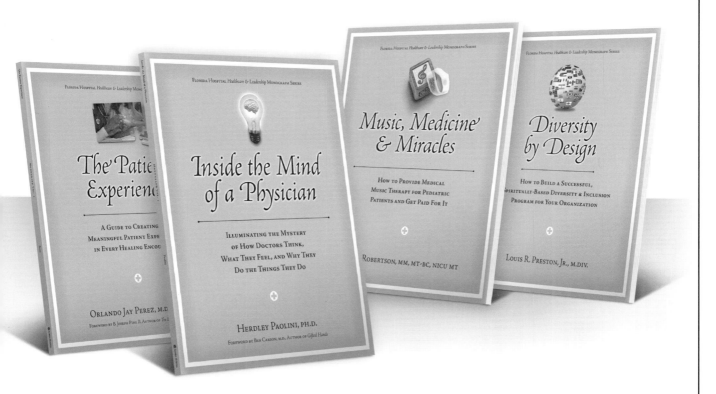

HEAR MORE FROM AMY ROBERTSON

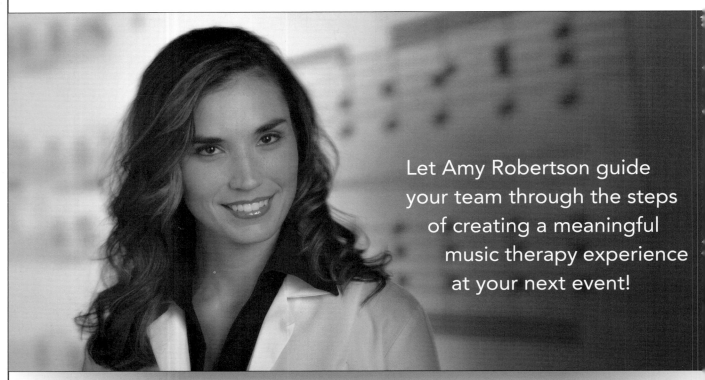

Let Amy Robertson guide your team through the steps of creating a meaningful music therapy experience at your next event!